Catholicism: A Very Short Introduction

VERY SHORT INTRODUCTIONS are for anyone wanting a stimulating and accessible way into a new subject. They are written by experts, and have been translated into more than 45 different languages.

The series began in 1995, and now covers a wide variety of topics in every discipline. The VSI library now contains over 500 volumes—a Very Short Introduction to everything from Psychology and Philosophy of Science to American History and Relativity—and continues to grow in every subject area.

Very Short Introductions available now:

ACCOUNTING Christopher Nobes
ADOLESCENCE Peter K. Smith
ADVERTISING Winston Fletcher
AFRICAN AMERICAN RELIGION
  Eddie S. Glaude Jr
AFRICAN HISTORY John Parker and
  Richard Rathbone
AFRICAN RELIGIONS Jacob K. Olupona
AGEING Nancy A. Pachana
AGNOSTICISM Robin Le Poidevin
AGRICULTURE Paul Brassley and
  Richard Soffe
ALEXANDER THE GREAT
  Hugh Bowden
ALGEBRA Peter M. Higgins
AMERICAN HISTORY Paul S. Boyer
AMERICAN IMMIGRATION
  David A. Gerber
AMERICAN LEGAL HISTORY
  G. Edward White
AMERICAN POLITICAL HISTORY
  Donald Critchlow
AMERICAN POLITICAL PARTIES
  AND ELECTIONS L. Sandy Maisel
AMERICAN POLITICS Richard M. Valelly
THE AMERICAN PRESIDENCY
  Charles O. Jones
THE AMERICAN REVOLUTION
  Robert J. Allison
AMERICAN SLAVERY
  Heather Andrea Williams
THE AMERICAN WEST Stephen Aron
AMERICAN WOMEN'S HISTORY
  Susan Ware
ANAESTHESIA Aidan O'Donnell

ANARCHISM Colin Ward
ANCIENT ASSYRIA Karen Radner
ANCIENT EGYPT Ian Shaw
ANCIENT EGYPTIAN ART AND
  ARCHITECTURE Christina Riggs
ANCIENT GREECE Paul Cartledge
THE ANCIENT NEAR EAST
  Amanda H. Podany
ANCIENT PHILOSOPHY Julia Annas
ANCIENT WARFARE Harry Sidebottom
ANGELS David Albert Jones
ANGLICANISM Mark Chapman
THE ANGLO-SAXON AGE John Blair
ANIMAL BEHAVIOUR
  Tristram D. Wyatt
THE ANIMAL KINGDOM
  Peter Holland
ANIMAL RIGHTS David DeGrazia
THE ANTARCTIC Klaus Dodds
ANTISEMITISM Steven Beller
ANXIETY Daniel Freeman and
  Jason Freeman
THE APOCRYPHAL GOSPELS
  Paul Foster
ARCHAEOLOGY Paul Bahn
ARCHITECTURE Andrew Ballantyne
ARISTOCRACY William Doyle
ARISTOTLE Jonathan Barnes
ART HISTORY Dana Arnold
ART THEORY Cynthia Freeland
ASIAN AMERICAN HISTORY
  Madeline Y. Hsu
ASTROBIOLOGY David C. Catling
ASTROPHYSICS James Binney
ATHEISM Julian Baggini

For more information visit our website

www.oup.com/vsi/

Gerald O'Collins

CATHOLICISM

A Very Short Introduction

SECOND EDITION

OXFORD
UNIVERSITY PRESS

Great Clarendon Street, Oxford, OX2 6DP,
United Kingdom

Oxford University Press is a department of the University of Oxford.
It furthers the University's objective of excellence in research, scholarship,
and education by publishing worldwide. Oxford is a registered trade mark of
Oxford University Press in the UK and in certain other countries

© Gerald O'Collins 2017

The moral rights of the author have been asserted

First edition published 2008
Second edition published 2017

Published in the United States of America by Oxford University Press
198 Madison Avenue, New York, NY 10016, United States of America

British Library Cataloguing in Publication Data
Data available

Library of Congress Control Number: 2016960541

ISBN 978-0-19-879685-5

Printed and bound by CPI Group (UK) Ltd, Croydon, CR0 4YY

Contents

Preface

As much as ever, images express and even shape history, including the story of the Catholic Church and its popes. Those who followed the April 2016 visit of Pope Francis to a refugee camp on the Greek island of Lesbos will recall how he brought home to the Vatican City three Muslim couples and their six children. These families had fled from Syria after their homes had been destroyed and their lives put at great risk. Francis waited at the foot of the stairs to welcome each one of them when they disembarked from the Alitalia flight at Fiumicino airport.

Many remember earlier images of Pope Francis kneeling before young men and women imprisoned in gaols and washing their feet on Holy Thursday. He does not beat the drum about being faithful to the teaching of the Second Vatican Council (1962–5). But in what he repeatedly does and says he remains true to the Council's deep concern to serve the poor, care for the suffering, and preach the good news that Jesus revealed and embodied for all time.

The pope's option for the poor had become blatantly clear when in July 2013 he made his first official journey out of Rome by flying south to visit Lampedusa. Shortly before he arrived, a boat carrying 165 asylum seekers from Eritrea pulled into the harbour of the tiny island. Francis celebrated the Eucharist, the sacred rite that commemorates the 'Last Supper' at which Jesus presided on the night before his crucifixion. As a setting for the religious service the pope chose a sports field that served as a reception centre for thousands of desperate people fleeing across the Mediterranean. His chalice had been carved out of the wood of a migrant ship, and the altar was a small, painted boat. After the service he laid a wreath in the harbour to recall the thousands of migrants and refugees who have drowned trying to reach Lampedusa. In his homily Pope Francis spoke out against 'the culture of comfort which makes us think only of ourselves' and remains 'insensitive to the cries of other people'. He added: 'in this globalized world we have fallen into globalized indifference'.

Three major documents have expressed the vision of Pope Francis. In *Evangelii Gaudium* ('the Joy of the Gospel' of 2013) he has invited 'all Christians, everywhere, to a renewed personal encounter with Jesus Christ'. He knows that 'the joy of the Gospel' will 'fill the hearts and lives of all who encounter Jesus' (nos. 1, 3). He wants Catholics and other Christians to lead the way in caring for our common home, the earth. His 2015 encyclical letter on ecology and the climate, *Laudato Si'* ('Praise be [to you, my Lord]'), denounces the widespread degradation of the environment caused by human greed and thoughtlessness. The exhortation Francis published in March 2016, *Amoris Laetitia* ('the Joy of Love'), proves at 256 pages the longest papal document ever to appear. It aims at promoting 'love in the family'. In his warm, down-to-earth style, he proposes ways for couples to remain in love for a lifetime and bring up their children wisely and happily. He knows that the family is the essential basis for the wellbeing of Christianity and of society at large. He wants couples to find something good and beautiful in the institution of marriage, because they are convinced that it makes a profound difference in their lives together.

Amoris Laetitia has appeared, however, at a time when many couples are reluctant to commit themselves to marriage.

The scandal of sexual abuse of minors perpetrated by priests and male religious has in many places robbed the Catholic Church of credibility. A loss of trust has led young people to decline the Church's blessing on their union. Indifference to the claims of the state means that many do not even attend a registry office to contract a civil marriage.

Landmark events in world history affect Pope Francis, Catholics, and all human beings alike. Recently such events have included Barack Obama serving as the forty-fourth president of the United States (2009–17), Vladimir Putin, who had been president of Russia (2000–8), returning as president in May 2012, and Donald Trump being elected US president. In Europe, North America, and other parts of the world, innumerable people of various faiths or of no religious belief continue to suffer from the impact of the 2007–8 financial crisis and the 'inequality which is the root of social ills' (*Evangelii Gaudium*, 202). They have also experienced effects of economic changes in China and India (the most populous countries in the world) and in Brazil (the largest Catholic country in the world).

In Africa and Asia, straight-out wars—or at least insurgency—have continued: in Afghanistan (which since 1979 has suffered nearly four decades of war and become one of the largest sources of the world's over sixty-five million refugees, asylum seekers, and internally displaced persons); in the Central African Republic (which has plunged into anarchy); in the Democratic Republic of the Congo (where the Second Congo War and its aftermath have caused well over five million deaths since 1998); and in Syria (where since 2011 armed conflict has resulted in over 300,000 deaths and eleven million people fleeing their homes).

A 2003 invasion (firmly opposed by Pope John Paul II) ravaged Iraq, and the country still does not enjoy internal peace. The same holds true of Libya after the fall of Colonel Muammar Gaddafi in 2011. After two decades of civil war, South Sudan gained independence in the same year, but like neighbouring Somalia does not yet enjoy a stable peace. After twenty-seven years of fighting, the defeat of the Tamil Tigers in May 2009, and some massacres, Sri Lanka is free of armed conflict.

These wars affect the current story of Catholic Christianity: for instance, in the Middle East, where many members of ancient Christian communities have fled their countries for safety. Catholics and other Christians remain widely involved in caring for refugees and displaced persons through such organizations as Caritas International, the Jesuit Refugee Service, and Malteser International. In Egypt, Pakistan, and other countries, militant Muslims continue to attack Christians and destroy their churches. On 29 April 2016, the Trevi Fountain in Rome was bathed in red light to honour contemporary Christian martyrs and an estimated 200 million Christians who currently suffer persecution. A month earlier four nuns, members of Mother Teresa's Missionaries of Charity who ran an old people's home in Yemen, were murdered along with several of the residents. In Iraq, Christians numbered over a million before the 2003 invasion. They are now less than 300,000 and decreasing every month.

Since I published the first edition of this book in 2008, the world's population has expanded to 7.4 billion by March 2016, and is still on the rise. Not only in Africa and Asia but also in Europe, the followers of Islam continue to grow and are moving towards the 2,000 million mark. This is still less than the total number of Christians but more than the number of Catholics, who with over 1,200 million make up more than half of all Christians. In the decade ending March 2016, Catholics in Asia rose by 20 per cent and in Africa by 41 per cent.

In the North Atlantic world, which includes not only Europe and North America but also outposts in Australia, New Zealand, and elsewhere, secular individualism continues to erode inherited Christian values by promoting abortion, same-sex marriage, and the 'right' to suicide. In 2014 Belgium offered a spectacular example of this trend by legalizing euthanasia for teenagers and even children. Such 'liberal' secularism in countries where the birth rate sometimes will not replace the current population stands in sharp contrast with the religious and ethical commitments of fast-growing Islam.

Even if the HIV/AIDS pandemic has been partially checked around the world, Russia has around one million cases. Sub-Saharan Africa remains the most affected region. In Uganda and elsewhere, Catholics and other Christians have stood tall in working against the pandemic and assisting those already infected.

The death of John Paul II in April 2005, the succession of Benedict XVI, his resignation in February 2013, and the election of Pope Francis, the first Latin American pope ever, have shaped the history of Catholicism. Francis leads the Church at a time when, at least in many Western countries, faith is no longer supported by culture. In the pre-modern world, religion had been the assumed and culturally reinforced basis for society. The post-Christian world has eroded a sense of belonging and promoted isolated individualism. The 'spiritual' has been divorced from the religious. Those who define themselves by saying 'I'm not religious, I'm spiritual' finish up having little or nothing to say to the secular world. The challenge facing Francis and, indeed, all practising Christians is that of connecting people's spiritual experience with the revealed word of God and the sacramental life of the community. The internet and other forces spread everywhere the non-religious, privatized mindset of the Western world; the challenge has gone global for Catholics and other Christians.

'Catholicity' belongs, of course, among the characteristics of the Church confessed by all Christians in the Nicene-Constantinopolitan Creed, a concise version of the Christian faith derived in its full form from the First Council of Constantinople (AD 381). Used at least sometimes every year by all Christians when they celebrate the Eucharist, this Creed expresses faith in the 'one, holy, *catholic*, and apostolic Church'. Some readers would prefer to give this book the title of *Roman Catholicism*. After all, Catholics are those Christians who accept the universal authority of the pope who lives in the Vatican and presides over the diocese of Rome. Nevertheless, when one speaks or writes of 'Catholics' or 'Catholicism', people almost invariably presume a reference to Roman Catholics. That surely was the presumption behind the invitation to write a Very Short Introduction to *Catholicism*, and not to *Roman Catholicism*.

In any case, many elements of Catholic Christianity are found beyond the Catholic Church: for example, the practice of baptism, the acceptance as normative of the Four Gospels and the letters of Paul, and government by bishops. What is distinctive about Catholicism need not always be uniquely Catholic. Greek, Russian, and other Orthodox Christians share with Catholics the seven sacraments: baptism, confirmation, the Eucharist, penance or reconciliation after sin, anointing of the sick, ordination, and matrimony. (Sacraments are outward and visible ceremonies, such as using water in baptism, that signify inward, spiritual gifts from God.)

This book aims at a wide readership among all those who for various reasons want to learn more about the Catholic Church. I write this book 'from the inside', as one who was born into a Catholic family and has tried to serve the Catholic and wider community as an ordained priest and teacher of theology. Identifying with the common faith and deep values of other Catholics, I hope to describe and explain Catholicism competently, but without becoming defensive and falsely 'biased'. Some 'insiders' show an unacceptable bias, but certainly not all. When it comes to music or drama, insiders who have years of study, experience, and commitment behind them can guide us happily through musical and dramatic compositions. In such areas, detached outsiders may be able to communicate a wealth of facts, but at times their judgements remain superficial.

Catholic worship, belief, and practice have been subject to changes that have embodied both healthy and faithful development and real corruption. How should one construe the ups and downs, the decay and renewal, the happy advances and the tragic disappointments of Catholics through the centuries? The first two chapters of this book offer an extended tour of that history. Then follow chapters that describe the central beliefs of Catholics about God and the human condition (Chapter 3); the Church and her sacramental life (Chapter 4); and her moral life and teaching (Chapter 5). The book will close by summarizing certain basic characteristics of Catholicism (Chapter 6), and presenting some urgent issues that confront Catholicism and its future (Chapter 7).

In telling the story of Catholicism, every attempt to generalize is constantly beset with enough exceptions to break the rule. But some generalizations find considerable support: the coexistence from the beginning of holiness and sinfulness; the recurrent tensions between local communities and a centralized institution; the Catholic Church's challenges to prevailing cultures along with widespread assimilation of them; and shifting relations between governments and the Church.

I dedicate this new edition to Paolo Dall'Oglio, SJ, abducted on 29 July 2013 in Syria and presumably now dead.

Gerald O'Collins, SJ, AC

Jesuit Theological College, Parkville, Australia
Christmas 2016

Abbreviations

Dei Verbum (the Word of God) Vatican II, Dogmatic Constitution on Divine Revelation, 1965

Gaudium et Spes (Joy and Hope) Vatican II, Pastoral Constitution on the Church in the Modern World, 1965

Lumen Gentium (the Light of the Nations) Vatican II, Dogmatic Constitution on the Church, 1964

Nostra Aetate (In Our Age) Vatican II, Declaration on the Relation of the Church to Non-Christian Religions, 1965

Sacrosanctum Concilium (the Sacred Council) Vatican II, Constitution on the Sacred Liturgy, 1963

Unitatis Redintegratio (the Restoration of Unity) Vatican II, Decree on Ecumenism, 1964

List of illustrations

Chapter 1
From Pentecost to Christopher Columbus (AD 30–1492)

In Rome and around the world, Pope Francis continues to show the face of Catholicism to the world. But was there, from the origins of Christianity, a recognizable entity that we might call the nascent Catholic Church? Can we identify, right from the first Pentecost (the Jewish feast when the Holy Spirit descended upon 120 disciples of Jesus (Acts 2: 1–4)), some kind of institution whose history could be written? By answering yes to these questions, this chapter opens the story of Catholic Christianity in Jerusalem after the resurrection of the crucified Jesus (most likely in April AD 30) and the outpouring of the Holy Spirit.

After Pentecost

During his public ministry, Jesus led a revival movement that remained largely within Judaism itself but had some surprising features: above all, his scandalous claim to a personal authority that put him on a par with the God whom he called 'Abba' (Father dear). From a wider group of disciples (who included some non-Jews), he chose a core group of twelve men (all Jews)—a gesture that indicated his intention to re-found the twelve tribes of Israel, or the Jewish nation descended from Abraham and Sarah.

The first Christians expected the risen Christ to return shortly in glory to judge the world. Totally focused on Jesus, they fashioned their interpretation and proclamation of him by putting together two elements: on the one hand, their experience of the events in which he had been the central protagonist and, on the other, what they continued to find relevant within Judaism. To articulate their convictions about Jesus and his role in fulfilling the divine purposes, they depended in part upon their Jewish heritage. Thus their initiation rite of baptism took over some values from purificatory rites of Judaism, not least from the baptism for the forgiveness of sins practised by John the Baptist. All the followers of Jesus continued to find in the Jewish psalms their main prayerbook. Some or even many of them continued to worship as Jews until excommunicated from Palestinian and other synagogues in the course of the 1st century. At least initially, Jesus' followers were unsure about the need to continue observing the Torah or Jewish law (especially about circumcision and dietary requirements) and the conditions they should impose on Gentiles who accepted faith in the crucified and risen Jesus. Yet the first Christians differed from other devout Jews by administering baptism 'in the name of Jesus' (e.g. Acts 2: 38) and celebrating together the Eucharist, the service in which bread and wine are consecrated and consumed (e.g. Acts 2: 42, 45).

In the Acts of the Apostles, Luke tells the story of the origin and early spread of Christian faith. In the opening chapters, Peter functions prominently as the head of the twelve apostles, the core group of public witnesses to Jesus' life, death, and resurrection. With his dramatic calling on the road to Damascus, Paul enters the Acts of the Apostles in ch. 9 and takes over the narrative from ch. 15. When Paul returns to Jerusalem in ch. 21, he meets James and 'all the elders'. But there is no mention of Peter still being in Jerusalem. Acts ends with Paul arriving in Rome several years before he and Peter died there as martyrs (between AD 64 and 67).

These first decades of Christian history featured the tension between two 'constituencies', the original Jerusalem Church with its vision of a Torah-observant community and the non-Torah-focused vision of Paul and others. The latter vision lifted the early Church beyond being merely a reform group within Judaism. Paul loved the Jerusalem community and showed that love by collecting money for them from other (local) churches (e.g. 2 Cor. 8: 1–9: 15). Nevertheless, a worldwide identity of Christians in Antioch, Rome, and further centres was formed in a tensional relationship with the Jerusalem community.

Paul spearheaded missionary activity around the Mediterranean world, and spread faith in Jesus as Lord and Saviour. Luke understands this original Christian expansion as opening up an indefinitely long period which will close when Jesus appears again in his glory. In the meantime, as Acts repeatedly indicates, the risen Jesus and his Holy Spirit constantly guide and empower Christian life and mission.

By the 60s, the followers of Jesus had come to be called 'Christians' (Acts 11: 26). Through baptism in the name of Jesus, they knew their sins to be forgiven, received the Holy Spirit, entered the community of the Church, and celebrated the Eucharist. When praying, they called on God as 'Abba' (Rom. 8: 15; Gal. 4: 6), and used not only the psalms but also the Lord's Prayer and other such prayers as the *Benedictus* and the *Magnificat* (Luke 1: 46–55, 68–79), which were originally in Greek like the rest of Luke's Gospel but were subsequently known by their Latin titles. They learned the teaching of Jesus that reached them through their apostolic leaders and their associates. They confessed the risen and exalted Jesus to be Messiah (anointed Deliverer), Lord, and Son of God, and to have sent them, together with God the Father, the gift of the Holy Spirit. They believed that the Spirit was offered to all peoples and that salvation no longer required circumcision and the practice of the Mosaic law in all its details (Acts 15: 1–35).

Paul's letters defend God's gift of salvation to all alike; justification is not gained through human efforts at fulfilling the Jewish law. Faith and baptism incorporate people into the Church, the Body of Christ, and put an end to distinctions between Jew and Gentile, slave and free, male and female (Gal. 3: 26–9). Faith in God the Father, in Jesus as Son of God and divine Lord, and in the Holy Spirit brings all believers together in the unity of baptism, the Eucharist, and a common life. The apostle insists that sharing in the one Eucharistic bread and in the one cup means belonging to the one Body of Christ (1 Cor. 10: 16–17).

While emphasizing the holy unity of the baptized, the apostle's letters let us glimpse the moral failures of early Christians. The First Letter to the Corinthians reveals how some suffered from factionalism, indulged doubts over the central truth of the resurrection, committed fornication, incest, and drunkenness, and showed a selfish unconcern for poorer Christians. The reproaches coming from Paul challenge illusions about a hypothetical golden age of Catholic Christianity that practised heroic ideals on all sides. From the outset, the Church suffered from scandals and divisions. The Book of Revelation, with its opening letters to the seven churches, joins the apostle in testifying to the mixture of holiness and sinfulness that characterized Christianity from the beginning (Rev. 2: 2–3: 22).

Along with holiness and sinfulness, a missionary outreach characterized early Christianity. The Acts of the Apostles and Paul's letters name missionaries who spread the good news about Jesus as Saviour of the world: Barnabas, Epaphroditus, Timothy, Titus, and, not least, Prisca (Priscilla) and Aquila. This married couple, when they lived in Ephesus and Rome, gathered believers in their home, and were also known to the Christians of Corinth (1 Cor. 16: 19; Acts 18: 2–3, 26). Paul calls this couple his 'fellow workers' (Rom. 16: 3).

Early leadership

In concluding his Letter to the Romans, Paul begins with 'our sister Phoebe, a deacon of the church', and writes of those who 'work' to spread the good news. The final chapter of Romans raises the question: was the Church meant to be a completely egalitarian community, free of any kind of subordination to office-holders? Did the vision of Jesus and the spontaneous direction of the Holy Spirit exclude such institutionalized leadership as came with the subsequent transmission of a threefold ministry of bishops, priests, and deacons? Did that historical development betray Jesus' original dream of male and female disciples as co-partners variously empowered by the Holy Spirit to minister to the whole community? Or was there always some kind of leadership that rightly developed and was handed on to successive generations for the good of all?

We find multiple evidence for the fact that Jesus chose twelve disciples from the wider ranks of his followers and gave them some kind of leadership role. Mark attests the original call and subsequent mission of the Twelve (Mark 3: 13–19; 6: 7–13). Q (*Quelle*, or 'source'), a collection of sayings of Jesus which both Matthew and Luke draw from, implies the existence of this core group (Matt. 19: 28 = Luke 22: 30). They experience an appearance of the risen Christ, a fact first attested by a traditional formula cited by Paul (1 Cor. 15: 5) and subsequently narrated in various ways by the Easter chapters of the Gospels. The Twelve are given authority by Christ to lead and teach in his name, a role for which, as Luke and (in his own way) John indicate, they are empowered by the Holy Spirit. Their apostolic mission shares in the mission of the Son and the Holy Spirit.

What do the Pauline letters indicate about leadership in the Church? A dramatic encounter with the risen Christ made Paul himself an apostle who proclaims the resurrection of the crucified Jesus (1 Cor. 9: 1–2; 15: 8–11; Gal. 1: 11–12, 15–17). Paul's sense of his own apostolic authority comes across clearly, not least in his Letter to the Galatians. After founding communities, he continues to lead them through his letters, messengers, and occasional visits. But how does he understand the authoritative ministry of others in the growing Church?

Paul notes how, within the whole 'Body of Christ', God has appointed various persons to be apostles, prophets, teachers, workers of miracles, healers, helpers, administrators, and speakers in different kinds of tongues (1 Cor. 12: 8–11, 18–30). The apostle's language in 1 Corinthians 12 has encouraged some to envisage a Spirit-filled community with no permanent institutions and ordained officers. But does Paul prescribe a Church order that sets personal gifts of the Spirit ('charisms') above any institutions and offices? It seems rather that he offers advice towards solving challenges facing the Corinthians' unity in Christ.

The foundation of many local churches by apostles and others brought a shift in leadership. Settled pastors (called 'overseers', 'elders', and 'deacons') took over from missionary apostles and other evangelists (see e.g. Acts 20: 17, 28; Phil. 1: 1; 1 Pet. 5: 1–4). The Pastoral Letters to Timothy and Titus, when recording a more developed organization of ministries, speak of 'overseers' or 'bishops' and their qualifications (1 Tim. 3: 1–7), of the 'elders' or 'presbyters' to be appointed by Titus 'in every town' (Titus 1: 5–6), and of the qualifications appropriate for 'deacons' (1 Tim. 3: 8–10, 12–13), and, apparently, also for 'deaconesses' (1 Tim. 3: 11). Much is stated about the teaching, preaching, administration, and domestic behaviour expected from leaders in the Church. But apart from some incidental regulations concerning worship (1 Tim. 2: 1–2, 8) and several references to the 'laying on of hands' (e.g. 1 Tim. 5: 22), nothing further is said about the religious ceremonies of the community or about the roles taken by leaders in baptizing, celebrating the Eucharist, and other rites of worship.

The New Testament supports the conclusion: Christian communities, both at the start (AD 30–70) and later in the 1st century (AD 70–100), were characterized by some organization. This organization, along with the basic equality of all the baptized, comprised the leaders (with their institutionalized offices) and the led (with their personal gifts). These communities were not simply and totally egalitarian.

We find in St Ignatius of Antioch (d. around AD 107) a key witness to the emerging structure of Catholic Christianity. The first writer known to have used the expression 'the Catholic Church' (*Epistle to the Smyrnaeans*, 8. 2), this martyr upheld worldwide, 'catholic' unity of belief and conduct. On the local scene, 'Catholicism' meant obedience to a bishop, supported by presbyters and deacons. The bishop was to preside at the celebration of the Eucharist, defend the centrality of Christ's bodily resurrection, and approve the marriage of Christians.

Irenaeus of Lyons (d. around AD 200) stressed continuity in the orthodox teaching of bishops, who succeeded one another after the time of the apostles. The succession of bishops could be traced back to the apostles—something Irenaeus did for the churches of Ephesus, Smyrna, and Rome, 'the greatest and oldest church' (*Adversus Haereses*, 3. 1-4). This championing of bishops as faithful teachers in the Church recognized the authority of the apostolic scriptures and rejected the new 'scriptures', produced by Gnostic movements that emerged after AD 150 on the margins of Christianity. Gnosticism drew on Jewish, Christian, and pagan sources to present salvation as involving not a resurrection of the body but the human spirit escaping from an evil, material world and returning to the heavenly world from which it had come.

Martyrdom

Persecution and martyrdom, inflicted particularly on Christian leaders, began very early. In AD 44 James the son of Zebedee was beheaded by the order of Herod Agrippa I. Paul lists the imprisonments, floggings, and other sufferings he had already undergone by the late 50s (2 Cor. 11: 23-7). Before his Damascus Road encounter with the risen Christ, he himself had acquiesced in the stoning of Stephen (Acts 7: 55-8: 1). In AD 62, the Jerusalem community lost its leader when James, a relative of Jesus, was stoned to death. Various records of martyrdoms have survived. In his *Annals* (15. 44), the Roman historian Tacitus tells the gruesome story of Christians killed by Emperor Nero:

> Covered with the skins of beasts, they were torn by dogs and perished; or were nailed to crosses; or were doomed to the flames and burnt, to provide illumination at night when there was no more daylight.

The *Passion of St Perpetua* describes how she and other Christians in Carthage were mauled by wild beasts and then had their throats cut in AD 203, during a persecution under Emperor Septimius Severus.

When Church leaders met for the First Council of Nicaea in AD 325, some of them showed the marks of persecution on their bodies. The hands of Paul of Neocaesarea had been paralysed by hot irons. Hosius, the bishop of Cordoba who acted as Emperor Constantine's adviser at the Council, and Eustathius, bishop of Antioch 324–30, had both suffered during the cruel persecution of Maximin Daza (d. 313). Two Egyptian bishops had each lost an eye. One of them, Paphnutius, had also been hamstrung. His scarred body evoked general veneration. Emperor Constantine showed respect by kissing his mutilated face.

Growth of Christianity

During the Roman persecution, many pagans owed their lives to Christian neighbours. By courageously caring for the sick, Christians saved numerous people during the epidemics of AD 165–80 and 251–66, which destroyed almost one-third of the population of the Roman world. These calamitous crises became the occasion for converting to the Church and being baptized.

Baptism 'in the name of the Father and of the Son and of the Holy Spirit', reported at the very end of Matthew's Gospel, became the standard formula for the basic rite of Christian initiation.

The *Didache*, written around AD 90 and so one of the earliest Christian works outside the New Testament, instructs those who baptize to use the Trinitarian formula (7. 1–3). The invocation of the Trinity provided the ground-plan for the questions ('Do you believe in God the Father?' and so forth) and answers that led to the formation of creeds, or brief summaries of Christian belief. With the Old Roman Creed crystallizing around the middle of the 3rd century, baptismal creeds developed in the West and the East and would be followed by the creed from the First Council of Nicaea (325).

The celebration of the Eucharist on Sunday, or the Lord's Day, reaches back to the start of Christianity. Since it was on that day that they first came to know of Jesus' resurrection from the dead, the earliest (Jewish) disciples moved their day of worship from the Jewish Sabbath to the Christian Sunday. Eucharistic worship comprised two parts: the Liturgy of the Word, which followed the pattern of synagogue services and consisted of prayers, hymns, and readings from the Bible, and the Liturgy of the Eucharist, which drew on Jesus' words at the Last Supper, included an invocation of the Holy Spirit (the *epiclesis*), and involved consecrating bread and wine into the body and blood of Christ.

The relationship with Judaism

Popular thinking often takes the destruction of Jerusalem in AD 70 to mark a definitive parting of the ways between the Church and Judaism. Yet in the 2nd century, Justin Martyr (who came from the Holy Land and died in Rome around AD 165) in his *Dialogue with Trypho* shared the Hebrew scriptures with the Jew Trypho and never belittled the faith of his debating partner.

A younger contemporary of Justin, Irenaeus of Lyons, set his face against the anti-Jewish aberrations of Marcion, who rejected the Creator God of the Old Testament as a cruel deity, not to be identified with the Father of our Lord Jesus Christ. Marcion excluded the Jewish scriptures and accepted only an emended version of Luke's Gospel and ten Pauline letters. Thus he wanted to strip Christianity both of its Jewish roots and of those Christian scriptures (in particular, Matthew's Gospel) that were concerned to justify Christian faith as fulfilling the Old Testament history and scriptures. Against such errors, Irenaeus championed not merely the four Gospels but also the enduring value of the Jewish scriptures and, in particular, their doctrine of God. There is only one God, who created the material world and made human beings in the divine image and likeness (Gen. 1: 27).

In the late 4th century, a section of *The Incarnation of the Word* (7. 33–40) by Athanasius shows how contact and debate with Jews still mattered to a bishop of Alexandria. And as a hermit in the Syrian desert, Jerome (d. AD 420) learned Hebrew from a Jewish scholar, enabling him to produce what came to be called the Vulgate, the most widely used Latin translation of the Bible; he translated the Hebrew scriptures directly from the original texts. But, sadly, by the end of the 4th century, this spirit of cooperation had changed: the misinterpretation of the cry of the crowd at Jesus' condemnation in Matthew 27: 25 ('his blood be on us and on our children'), the polemic against 'the Jews' in John's Gospel, some severe language from Paul (e.g. 1 Thess. 2: 14–16), and other texts and factors encouraged anti-Jewish attitudes among Christians. With John Chrysostom (d. AD 407), archbishop of Constantinople, anti-Jewish polemics set in. Catholics committed terrible crimes against Jews or remained guilty bystanders of such crimes. It would only be with Pope John XXIII (d. 1963), the Second Vatican Council (1962–5), and Pope John Paul II (d. 2005) that a clear change of direction came in teaching and practice. The Second Vatican Council called for repentance and denounced 'the hatred, persecutions, and displays of anti-Semitism directed against Jews at any time and from any source' (*Nostra Aetate*, 4).

Constantine and controversies

Constantine's victory of 28 October 312 on the outskirts of Rome made him the Emperor of the Western Empire. Before engaging the forces of Maxentius, his rival for power, Constantine reputedly had a vision of Christ's cross and the words: 'in this sign you will conquer'. With the sign of the cross on his own helmet and his soldiers' shields, he believed that the one, all-powerful God guaranteed the military triumph. The 313 Edict of Milan, a verbal agreement reached between Constantine and Licinius, the emperor of the Eastern Empire, pledged religious freedom for Christians and the restitution of goods confiscated from them during the severe persecution decreed by Emperor Diocletian in February 303 and continuing until 310.

Christians experienced a reversal of fortune when Constantine initiated a series of legislative acts in their favour. In March 321, he decreed Sunday to be a day of rest. In 324, public money became available for the construction of churches, and in 326 Constantine, encouraged by his elderly mother Helena (d. around 330), began building the central shrine of Christendom, the Church of the Resurrection in Jerusalem. He had already started building St Peter's Basilica in Rome, sited on the place of the apostle's burial, and completed in 328. (One should note, however, that Glen W. Bowersock and Richard Westall have proposed, respectively, 337–50 and 357–9 for the building of St Peter's Basilica.)

Visitors to St Peter's (reconstructed in the 16th and 17th centuries according to plans of Bramante, Raphael, Michelangelo, and other artistic geniuses) can stop in the portico to gaze at the statues of two emperors, each astride a horse: Constantine and Charlemagne (who was crowned in St Peter's on Christmas Day 800 as the first emperor of the Holy Roman Empire). Were they saviours or masters of the Church? However we judge their impact on

Christian life, Constantine, by tolerating and then encouraging Christianity, brought no separation of Church and state. He convened, funded, and (at least initially) presided at the first General Council, that of Nicaea in 325. He legislated for orthodox faith, outlawed heresy, and (even though he was not baptized until shortly before his death in 337) preached weekly sermons to his courtiers. Henceforth Christianity would continue to struggle with Church–state relations—under monarchies, dictatorships, oligarchies, democracies, and all manner of variants in these systems of government.

Toleration had hardly arrived under Constantine before Christians found themselves embroiled in the first of three major struggles for their faith in Christ.

First, Arius, a priest from Egypt, began spreading the notion that the Son of God was only a created being and hence did not share in the eternal existence of the Father. The bishops at the First Council of Nicaea (325), also called Nicaea I, defended the divine identity of the Son and declared him to be 'true God from true God, begotten, not made, of one being/substance with the Father'. The Council left indelibly printed on the conscience of Catholics (and other Christians) a deep faith in the divinity of Christ. This faith remained for them a non-negotiable truth.

Then, within fifty years, Apollinarius, a bishop of Laodicaea (in Asia Minor), began defending a position at the other extreme from Arius. Intent on defending the Nicene faith in Christ's divinity, Apollinarius maintained that in the incarnation the Logos, or Word of God, assumed a living body but took the place in Christ of the higher (rational) soul. Hence Apollinarius did not accept a complete humanity in Christ: he was truly divine but, by lacking a rational soul, he was not fully human. By condemning Apollinarius, the First Council of Constantinople (381), also called Constantinople I, upheld the complete humanity that the Word of God had assumed.

Granted that Christ is truly divine (Nicaea I) and fully human (Constantinople I), how is the *union* between his divinity and humanity to be understood? The Council of Ephesus (431) taught that his divinity and humanity are not *separated*, as if Christ were divided into two agents: the Word of God and the man Jesus. Twenty years later, the Council of Chalcedon (451) added that the divinity and humanity of Christ (his two 'natures') are not merged together but remain truly *distinct*. The one person of Christ existed and exists in two complete (distinct but not separate) natures, with all the attributes that belong essentially to those two natures.

The break between East and West

Across the Bosphorus from Constantinople, Chalcedon was at the heart of the Eastern (Roman) Empire. But a contribution to the Council's teaching came from the West, through a letter from Pope Leo I. At Chalcedon, more than 500 bishops approved this letter from 'the most blessed and most holy Archbishop Leo...since it agrees with the confession of the great [St] Peter and is a pillar of support to all against the heterodox'. A year later, it was Leo the Great who persuaded Attila, king of the Huns and known as 'the Scourge of God', not to sack Rome. In the next century, Gregory the Great (pope 590–604) did much to re-found Catholic Christianity in Britain by sending St Augustine to England, where he landed in Kent during the summer of 597. There were difficulties between this somewhat timid monk and representatives of the ancient Celtic Church. But the success of Augustine's mission was sealed when he was consecrated the first archbishop of Canterbury. An English Christianity emerged that happily mingled Anglo-Saxon, Celtic, and Roman elements.

Five months after his election to the papacy, Gregory the Great in a circular letter of February 591 to five Eastern patriarchs declared that he venerated the first four Councils (Nicaea I, Constantinople I, Ephesus, and Chalcedon), just as he venerated the four Gospels.

Even late in the day, his endorsement of Constantinople I (381), and the Creed it developed on the basis of Nicaea I, definitively clarified the status of that second Council for the universal Church and showed a proper sensitivity to East–West relations. Since none of its bishops had taken part in Constantinople I, the Western Church had been slow to recognize the authority of that council and its Creed.

By the late 9th century, Eastern theologians began accusing Western Catholics of unilaterally tampering with the Nicene-Constantinopolitan Creed by adding the 'Filioque', or teaching about the Holy Spirit 'proceeding' not only from the Father but also from the Son. Charlemagne (d. 814) accepted these fateful words (that had been added earlier, probably at the Fourth Synod of Braga (675)) when he encouraged the chanting of the Creed at Mass throughout his empire. The addition was eventually adopted in Rome when Emperor Henry II in 1013 ordered the Latin Church everywhere to insert the 'Filioque' when they sang or recited the Creed.

For a century or more, few outstanding popes had been elected. Sergius III (pope 904–11) was said to have murdered his two predecessors, and John XII (pope 955–64) was given the papal office at the age of 20 through the influence of his powerful father. Between 882 and 984, nine popes were murdered by poison, strangulation, and other methods. That was the darkest hour of the papacy, which appalled even the dissolute world of 10th-century Rome. This deplorable period also helped trigger a lasting schism between Western Catholicism and Orthodox (Greek for 'right belief') Christianity, a break conventionally dated to a day in 1054 when the patriarch of Constantinople and the leader of a delegation from Rome mutually excommunicated one another.

The schism between East and West was, however, never complete; a minority of Eastern-rite Christians remained in communion with the bishop of Rome. Yet the split encouraged a Western, over-centralized system focused on the pope rather than normal governance through regional synods or assemblies of bishops—the system that characterizes Eastern Christianity.

Bishops, monks, and missionaries

Catholic and other Christians have never stopped finding inspiration from many bishops, monks, and missionaries who led and spread the Church in the first millennium and beyond. St Augustine (354–430), bishop of Hippo in North Africa, was the first and, arguably, the greatest of an 'A' team of three theologians who moulded Western Catholic thought. The other two are St Anselm (d. 1109 as archbishop of Canterbury) and the priest and Dominican professor St Thomas Aquinas (d. 1274).

Monasticism may be described as a movement among baptized Christians who respond to Christ's call to perfection by giving themselves, through poverty, celibacy, and obedience, to a life of prayer, worship in common, and the service of others. In the 4th century, St Basil of Caesarea (d. 379) and his sister St Macrina the Younger (d. around 380) contributed to the rise of Eastern monasticism. That in turn helped the rise of Western monasticism. St Benedict of Nursia (d. around 550), after living as a hermit in a cave at Subiaco (outside Rome), gathered followers and founded twelve monastic communities, each with twelve monks and an abbot appointed by Benedict. His sister, St Scholastica (d. around 543), who founded a convent a few miles from Monte Cassino, is buried in the same grave as her brother. Their monastic way of life proved a haven in an unsettled society, and helped to preserve the literature and art forms from the Graeco-Roman culture.

Despite invasions of Germanic and other northern tribes, sacred and secular learning remained alive, thanks to such leaders as St Hilda of Whitby (d. 680), St Bede 'the Venerable' (d. 735), and many other men and women who followed the monastic way of life. Dated from around 800, the glorious writing and illustrations of the Book of Kells (from a monastery in County Meath but preserved in Trinity College, Dublin) set forth the four Gospels. That manuscript glows like a jewel in bearing witness to the monastic love for the scriptures, in general, and for the life of Christ, in particular.

Apparently born in Roman Britain, St Patrick (d. around 461) spent six years as a slave in Ireland before escaping back to Britain. After training for Christian ministry, he returned to Ireland as a bishop, made Armagh his episcopal see, and set himself to evangelize the whole island. The daughter of one couple he baptized, St Brigid (d. around 523), founded at Kildare the first nunnery in Ireland and influenced the growth of Catholic Christianity.

In the 6th century, large monastic communities began to grow in Ireland, and for many centuries ecclesiastical authority was exercised by the abbots (and abbesses) of these monasteries. Some abbots, like St Columba (d. 597) and St Columbanus (d. 615), left Ireland and became missionaries abroad: the former in Scotland and the latter in Gaul, Switzerland, and northern Italy. These Celtic monk-missionaries, along with their Anglo-Saxon counterparts, established new monasteries—such as Columba's foundation on the Island of Iona, off the Scottish coast—and spread the practice of 'private' penance or 'auricular' (in the ear) confession of sins. Eventually such private confession of sins became standard and replaced the original system of public penance.

Cathedrals, religious orders, and pilgrimages

Any account of Catholicism from the 11th to the 15th century will concentrate on Europe, as that is where the overwhelming majority of Catholics then lived. But the discovery of the Americas in 1492 by Christopher Columbus (1451–1506) and subsequent events would make the situation dramatically different at the end of the 20th century. By the year 2000, three-quarters of the world's one billion Catholics were living in the Americas (North, Central, and South), Africa, Asia, and Oceania.

Church buildings from the 11th to the 16th century witness to the Catholicism of those centuries, when all classes of society collaborated to express their faith through mosaics, carvings, paintings, stained-glass windows, and the churches and monasteries that housed them. From around AD 1000 until the 13th century, Romanesque style (and its variant in Norman style) dominated—with massive walls, relatively small windows, and round arches and vaults. The Romanesque basilica of Vézelay (south-east of Paris), Durham Cathedral, and the Norman (with Arab decoration) Abbey of Monreale, near Palermo, offer outstanding examples from those centuries. The 12th-century mosaics of Monreale represent an entire cycle of Old Testament and New Testament stories and figures, with a majestic Christ enthroned in the central apse.

Gothic style began with the royal Abbey Church of Saint-Denis (near Paris), which was dedicated in 1144. Pointed arches, soaring towers, and the light that streamed through the walls of brilliant stained glass lifted human minds and hearts to God. The Gothic cathedrals of Chartres (begun 1145; Figure 1) and Amiens (begun 1220) became models for churches right across Europe. The rich sculpture, stained glass, and luminous structure of Chartres Cathedral (south-west of Paris) have always inspired superlatives.

Along with the visible heritage of Catholicism, one should not forget the musical life that flourished in Eastern and Western worship. The worship of Eastern Christians, whether Orthodox or Catholic, is enriched by liturgical hymns, some as old as the 5th century. The medieval repertoire of plainchant and the glory

1. Famous for its stained-glass windows and exterior sculptures, Chartres embodies Gothic cathedrals at their best and humanity rising towards God.

of polyphony belong among the treasures of Western civilization, and have enjoyed an extraordinary revival.

From the time of the Emperor Charlemagne, Benedictine abbeys spread across Europe, but by medieval times some had lost their original fervour. A reform movement led to the foundation of new communities where stricter observance prevailed. The Cistercian Order emerged, its name coming from its mother house in Cîteaux, where St Bernard (1090–1153) became a novice in 1112. His influence played a major part in disseminating the new order right across Western Europe. By the close of the 12th century, 530 Cistercian abbeys had been established, and there would be a further 150 foundations in the next century. Bernard sent a group of monks to found the Abbey of Rievaulx in Yorkshire. By the time of St Aelred (abbot 1147–67, and called the 'Bernard of the North'), this community numbered around 600 monks. Like Rievaulx, Cistercian houses were normally erected in remote areas. They followed strict rules about silence, diet, and manual labour, fostered plain architecture, and practised efficient farming methods.

Along with reactions to decadence, a new, tender devotion to Jesus in his humanity worked to encourage fresh initiatives in religious life. Where the Cistercians represented a 'flight from the world', the 'mendicant' ('living by begging') orders of Dominicans and Franciscans also revitalized medieval Catholicism but in different ways.

St Dominic (d. 1221), the founder of the Order of Preachers (commonly called the Dominicans), worked untiringly to spread true Christian doctrine. A courageous and efficient leader, he parted ways with the careerism of many upwardly mobile priests by three times refusing to accept nomination as a bishop. Dominican preachers popularized the practice of the rosary, still a very common devotion among Catholics and some other Christians. It commemorates events involving Christ or his mother Mary and requires a string of beads to count the particular prayers it involves. The five 'joyful mysteries' centre on Christ's birth and childhood. The (recently added) five 'mysteries of light' begin with Christ's baptism and end with his institution of the Eucharist. The five 'sorrowful mysteries' open with Christ's agony in the garden and end with his death on the cross. The five 'glorious mysteries' start with Christ's resurrection and close with Mary's sharing in her Son's victory over death. Each mystery includes the 'Our Father' (once), the 'Hail Mary' (ten times), and the 'Glory be to the Father' (once).

The Dominicans propagated the rosary; the Franciscans did the same for the Christmas crib and the Stations of the Cross (a devotion in which the participants pray as they move around fourteen scenes from the suffering and death of Christ). These devotions flowed straight out of the very Jesus-centred life of St Francis of Assisi (d. 1226). By celebrating Christmas in a barn with animals and straw, Francis conveyed the deep meaning of Jesus' birth and initiated the practice of using various figures to construct what we know as Christmas cribs or crèches. During an ecstatic experience two years before his death, Francis received the stigmata—wounds on his hands, feet, and side that corresponded to those of the crucified Jesus and so completed the Christ-like image he presented. The followers of Francis took over in 1342 the custody of the shrines in Jerusalem associated with Christ's suffering and crucifixion. For those Christians unable to visit the Holy Land, Franciscans led the way in erecting innumerable Stations of the Cross as a means for sharing through prayer in the passion, death, and burial of Jesus.

The influence of Francis and his associate, St Clare (1194–1253), has endured through such figures as St Antony of Padua (1195–1231), St Angela of Foligno (d. 1309), St ('Padre') Pio of Pietralcina (1887–1968), and other Franciscan mystics and missionaries. The humility, total poverty, and Christ-like love practised by Francis have made him one of the most popular saints of all time.

2. Pilgrims honouring the Virgin Mary at the shrine of Lo Vásquez, Chile.

At the age of 35, Dante Alighieri (1265–1321) joined other pilgrims in Rome for the 'Jubilee Year' of 1300, the first of twenty-six Jubilee Years that have brought Catholics to Rome down to 2000. These Jubilee Years offer particular spiritual benefits to those who come on pilgrimage to Rome and perform various religious exercises. Pilgrimages stretch back to the origins of the Jewish-Christian story (Figure 2). Abraham and Sarah left Ur of the Chaldees and became nomads for God. New Testament books such as the Letter to the Hebrews and the First Letter of Peter saw human life as a journey to the heavenly homeland. By AD 250, the cult of Peter and Paul began to flourish in Rome and drew pilgrims to their tombs. A work from the end of the 4th century, the *Pilgrimage of Etheria*, told the story of a Christian woman (probably a Spaniard) who visited Jerusalem and its neighbourhood. She described the liturgical ceremonies: not only the daily and Sunday offices but also the services for the Epiphany, Holy Week (including the procession of palms to the Mount of Olives, and the veneration of the cross), Easter, and Pentecost.

Dante used the pilgrimage theme to open the *Divine Comedy* ('In the middle of our life's road I found myself in a dark wood—the straight way ahead lost'); the spiritual transformation of the pilgrim takes him through hell and purgatory to heaven. Along with Jerusalem and Santiago de Compostela (with its tomb of St James the Apostle), Rome has continued to attract pilgrims, especially during Jubilee Years. Pope Francis wanted the Extraordinary Jubilee of Mercy (8 December 2015–20 November 2016) to be celebrated not only in Rome but also in other centres around the world.

Not as exalted a poet as Dante, Geoffrey Chaucer (1340–1400) pictured in *The Canterbury Tales* twenty-nine pilgrims on their way to the shrine of St Thomas Becket (d. 1170) in Canterbury Cathedral. This group of men and women allowed Chaucer to describe the saints and sinners who made up the Catholic Church of his day. Those shared journeys to the shrines of saints embodied a common faith. The ancient Celts named such shrines 'thin places'; time and again, they experienced there close communication with God. Pilgrimages reinforced the consciousness of life as a spiritual journey, a preparation for death and eternal life. In later centuries, pilgrimages have also played a role in maintaining a sense of national identity. Thus, for example, devotion to the Blessed Virgin Mary at her shrine of Czestochowa continues to shape Catholicism in Poland. This shrine was visited by many foreigners who came to nearby Kraków for the World Youth Day (25–31 July 2016).

The Crusades

After the scandalous low of the 10th-century papacy, the second thousand years of Catholicism began with Sylvester II (pope 999–1003), a pope committed to promoting the healthy state of the Church. A longer papacy allowed Gregory VII (pope 1073–85) to work more vigorously towards reforming money-hungry and sexually immoral clergy and opposing secular rulers who meddled in the election of bishops and similar matters. The Gregorian reforms, while being on balance praiseworthy, suffered from their ambiguities, both within the Catholic Church and beyond. Within the Church, Gregory effected a certain shift of power from the local churches to the Roman See. Corrupt or inept officials of the popes could misuse this new centralism at the expense of the bishops in charge of dioceses.

Relations with 'others' featured in a letter of 1076 to Anzir, the Muslim king of Mauretania, whom Gregory thanked for freeing some prisoners and promising to free some more. Anzir had even sent a candidate to be consecrated a bishop and so take care of his Christian subjects. Nearly 900 years later, in its Declaration on the Relation of the Church to Non-Christian Religions, the Second Vatican Council recalled this letter, which had recognized how Christians and Muslims honour Abraham and adore the same God.

After the death of Muhammad in Medina (Arabia) in 632, the Arab conquests of Palestine, Syria, Egypt, and North Africa moved ahead fast. Christianity lost vast tracts to Islam. In the 8th century, Muslim forces conquered Spain and were stopped from overrunning the kingdom of the Franks by the victory won in 732 near Poitiers by the soldiers of Charles Martel, the grandfather of Charlemagne. Armed conflicts, as well as some religious and cultural dialogue, characterized Christian–Muslim relations in the centuries to come. The Muslim rulers of Spain normally tolerated Christians and Jews, especially in such cultural centres as Cordoba. An outstanding Arab philosopher and polymath, Averroes (1126–98), was born and lived there, and his commentaries on Aristotle exercised a considerable influence on Christian thinkers. The Jewish philosopher Moses Maimonides (1135–1204) was also born in Cordoba and eventually settled in Old Cairo. Writing in both Hebrew and Arabic, he affected such Christians as Thomas Aquinas by his *Guide for the Perplexed*, which synthesized divine revelation with the findings of human reason developed by

Aristotle. But the Crusades and the gradual reconquest of Spain by Christian princes harmed relations with Muslims and Jews.

In a speech delivered at Clermont (France) in 1095, Urban II (pope 1088–99), who had been made a cardinal by Gregory VII and continued his programme of reform, called for a Christian war to recapture the Holy Land from the Muslims. Within a few months the First Crusade was under way. When the Crusaders captured Jerusalem in 1099, they killed around 10,000 Muslims, as well as many Jews. This barbaric slaughter sent shock waves around the Mediterranean world. Christian minorities in Muslim countries experienced hardships they had not known before. In 1204, when the Fourth Crusade switched to Constantinople from its original objective (Egypt), the Crusaders sacked the city and set up the Latin Empire and patriarchate. They achieved only a temporary reunion between the Eastern and Western Churches. The long-term effect of the Fourth Crusade was to seal the schism between Rome and Constantinople and weaken the Eastern Empire against Muslim inroads.

A few years later, in 1236, Christian forces reconquered Cordoba. When Granada, the last Spanish territory held by the Muslims, surrendered in 1492, the new Christian Spain of Ferdinand and Isabella failed to incorporate a Muslim minority, as well as expelling its Jewish population. A few years earlier (1478), Ferdinand and Isabella had set up the Spanish Inquisition to prosecute heretical views and (sometimes) immoral behaviour. In certain cities, the Inquisition convicted over 40 per cent of those accused and handed them over to be burnt by the civil authorities. From the middle of the 16th century, the percentage of trials resulting in capital punishment had dropped to about 1 per cent. The use of torture, the anonymity of witnesses, and other features made the Inquisition enduringly notorious as an instrument of religious and civil control. Among its few redeeming features was the way that, unlike countries in northern Europe, it hardly ever concerned itself with witchcraft, since its officials normally did not believe that any such thing existed.

Not long before the reign of Ferdinand and Isabella began, the Ottoman Empire, founded around 1300 in Turkey, had captured (Christian) Constantinople in 1453. By the end of the 16th century, the Ottoman power extended from Hungary, through the Balkans and Greece, to Egypt. This new Muslim expansion into Europe was dealt a crushing blow, at least by sea, through the naval forces of the Christian League at the battle of Lepanto (near the Gulf of Corinth) in 1571. On the anniversary of the naval battle at Lepanto, Pope Pius V instituted the feast of Our Lady of the Rosary to be celebrated on 7 October. Catholics believed themselves to be victorious through the help of the Holy Mother of God, invoked by praying the rosary. The feast confirmed a trend among Spanish and other Catholics to define themselves, in part, by opposition to Muslims.

By the time of the battle of Lepanto, however, the expeditions of Christopher Columbus and the Protestant Reformation had changed forever the direction of Catholic and world history. We turn now to those changes.

Chapter 2
From Christopher Columbus to the present (1492–2017)

What has being Catholic meant over the last 500 years? To organize the themes, we will look in turn at the expansion of Europe, the Reformation, the new learning, and the coming of the world Church.

The expansion of Europe

The discoveries initiated by Columbus revealed the existence of millions of human beings in societies that had gone on for many centuries without the slightest chance of hearing about Jesus Christ and joining the Church. The arrival of the Europeans in the Americas raised the issue of universal participation in the benefits of Christ's redemption. How could he have been the Saviour for the indigenous peoples of the Americas? How could they have shared in his redemptive grace without even hearing his name?

In 1271–5, the Venetian Marco Polo visited China and provided the earliest European description of the Far East. This tale of the wealth of 'Cathay' fascinated later generations, including a Genovese sea captain, Christopher Columbus. He thought he could reach Asia when he sailed westward in 1492.

The start of the Western Age of Discovery pre-dates, however, Columbus' crossing of the Atlantic. The Portuguese Prince Henry the Navigator (1394–1460) promoted the exploration and colonization of the Canaries and the Azores. Under his patronage Portuguese seamen sailed down the west coast of Africa. In 1487, Bartolomeo Dias (d. 1500) became the first (known) European captain to round the Cape of Good Hope and so open up new sea routes to India and beyond. Within a few years of these Portuguese voyages and Columbus' discovery, Europeans began to circumnavigate the world, to map it, and to name it with European names ('Africa', 'America', 'Asia', and 'Australia'). Western and Christian domination were on the way.

Alexander VI (pope 1492–1503) divided the New World between Spain and Portugal, giving their kings sovereign power over the lands that their subjects were discovering and making them responsible for evangelizing the people of those lands. The Portuguese rulers developed an empire in Africa, America, and the Far East, and sent Catholic missionaries around the world. Apart from Angola, Mozambique, and such small enclaves as East Timor and Goa, the major lasting result of the Portuguese evangelization and colonization remains Brazil, currently the largest Catholic nation in the world; its population of over 205 million people (by 2015) is still predominantly Catholic.

Under Emperor Charles V, king of Spain from 1516 to 1556, the Spanish Empire spread through Central and South America. In 1521, Mexico fell to Hernándo Cortés; in 1530, Peru was conquered by Francisco Pizarro. Along with or shortly after the violent invasions and massacres committed by the *conquistadores*, Dominicans, Franciscans, and other missionaries arrived and preached the Christian message, sometimes by methods that failed to respect the freedom and religious sensitivities of the Aztecs of Mexico, the Incas of Peru, the Mayas of Yucatán, and other American Indians. Catholicism was established everywhere in Central and South America. Some groups, notably the Mexicans, embraced the new faith as a liberation from certain horrifying customs. The religion of the Aztecs had included human sacrifice, and many such sacrifices were rounded off by cannibalism, with members of the nobility eating the victims.

But the Indian societies were ravaged by invaders in search of gold and devastated by smallpox, other diseases, and alcoholism. The Indian population of Spanish-ruled America declined by at least 75 per cent in the first hundred years of that rule. The collapse of the local population led the *conquistadores* to import black slaves from Africa. Some religious leaders, such as Bartolomé de Las Casas (1474–1566), denounced the crimes committed in the name of Spain and Christianity. Significantly, this courageous Dominican served as bishop of Chiapas (1542–50), a poor diocese in southern Mexico where in the 1990s the Indian population hit world headlines over their struggle for civil and religious rights.

By 1620, thirty-six bishoprics and countless parishes in Central and South America served the Spanish settlers, Indian converts, and other groups, with everything under the control of two viceroys: one in Peru and the other in New Spain (Mexico). Through the viceroys the running of the colonial state and the organization of the Church depended upon Madrid. Popes had no control, for example, over the appointment of bishops.

One group that maintained its freedom from royal control was the Society of Jesus, which insisted on its primary obedience being to a superior general resident in Rome and through him to the pope. Besides developing colleges and churches in the towns, the Jesuits spread out among the Indian population where their frontier missionary work practised the peaceful methods of evangelization advocated by Las Casas. They sometimes succeeded in a remarkable way—as with the Guarani Indians of Paraguay. From 1603, they began settlements, which combined agricultural work, various crafts, and a style of worship that included much music. With the help of coadjutor brothers (non-ordained Jesuits), some of them ex-soldiers who had survived wars in Europe, the missionaries trained the Guaranis to defend themselves effectively against slave traders. The 1767 expulsion of Jesuits from Spanish America brought this missionary work to an end—as dramatically expressed in the film *The Mission* (1986). The ten settlements of the Chiquitos mission, in what became Bolivia, survived the loss of their spiritual leaders somewhat better. There the Jesuit mix of education, agriculture, and religious celebrations integrated even more skilfully the Indian language and culture with Christianity.

A few Jesuits, such as St Peter Claver (1580–1654), spent their lives courageously serving a very different group, the African slaves imported in ever-increasing numbers into Brazil, Cuba, Venezuela, and other lands of the Portuguese and Spanish empires. The slaves provided labour for the sugar plantations and other projects. But Claver enjoyed very little back-up. Many Jesuits and others ministered to the Indians, but the population of black slaves, often much worse treated, were totally subjected to their white owners. The black population came to accept Christianity but sometimes with a West African mix, as in the Afro-Brazilian cults. Catholic Brazil became the last country in the world to abolish slavery—only in 1888.

Out in Asia, missionaries such as St Francis Xavier (1506–52) reached India, Sri Lanka, Malacca, the Moluccas, and Japan. One of the first Europeans ever to visit Japan, he created Catholic communities there. Tragically, fear of foreign invasions triggered savage persecutions from the end of the 16th century. Thousands of Catholics suffered death for their faith; in 1640, Japan was closed to all foreigners and Christianity itself totally proscribed. When these restrictions were lifted in the second half of the 19th century, foreign missionaries discovered many hidden Catholics who had secretly kept and handed on their faith. Xavier himself had died on an island south of Canton, while waiting to enter China.

Within a few years of his death, however, other Jesuits entered China. Through his learning in astronomy, languages, and mathematics, the Italian Matteo Ricci (1552–1610) won the freedom to preach the Christian message. The German Jesuit Adam Schall (1591–1666) helped reform the Chinese calendar. By this and other achievements in astronomy (such as the prediction of an eclipse in 1629), the way was open for a Flemish Jesuit, Ferdinand Verbiest (1623–88), to be nominated president of the Chinese Imperial Board of Astronomy. This appointment by the Chinese ruling dynasty signalled the high point of a missionary endeavour that not only combined faith with human learning but also adapted Christian ceremonies to the local culture. This approach accommodated traditional Chinese rituals and beliefs, including the practice of venerating ancestors. The success of this accommodation gave rise to violent controversy over the 'Chinese rites'. In 1704, after a century of debate, Clement XI (pope 1700–21) was persuaded to condemn such adaptations as tainted by superstition. The Chinese emperors were outraged; during the 1720s, missionaries and then Christianity itself were banned in China. Eventually, 20th-century popes and the Second Vatican Council (1962–5) were to accept and even encourage adaptation to various cultures and a full role for the local clergy (Figure 3).

This full role came slowly in many places, notably in the Philippines. Evangelization by Dominican, Franciscan, and other missionaries followed the start of Spanish rule in 1565. Even though the majority of Filipinos had been baptized by the end of the 18th century, the indigenous clergy remained in inferior positions. It was only in 1905 that the first Filipino bishop was appointed. Pope Pius XI, however, encouraged local leadership. In 1926, he personally consecrated six Chinese bishops; in 1936, he appointed the first Japanese archbishop of Tokyo.

In West Africa, the horrors of the slave trade continued until the 1860s. By that time, Catholic, Protestant, and Anglican missionaries had begun serious evangelization of Africa south of the Sahara. In Italy, post-Napoleonic France, and elsewhere, a new enthusiasm grew to promote missions. Religious congregations with a specifically African focus, such as the Holy

3. Pope John XXIII is carried through St Peter's Square at the opening of the Second Vatican Council (1962–5), the most significant event in 20th-century Catholic history.

Ghost Fathers, the Society of African Missions, the White Fathers, the Verona Fathers, and the Missionary Sisters of Verona, came into existence. Through the 20th century, with the work of African laymen and -women, Catholicism grew enormously in Africa. Despite the wounds of colonialism, recurrent wars, corrupt rulers, and famines, by the year 2000, 175 million out of 350 million Christians in Africa were Catholics. The first two African Catholics to become bishops of dioceses were appointed in 1939. By the year 1990, there were over 350 such African bishops, many of them concerned with the task of indigenizing or inculturating Catholic rituals in their region.

A last wave of Catholic missionary expansion that should be recalled affected North America, Oceania, and other parts of the globe.

From the 19th century, congregations of missionary women played a major role in bringing Catholicism to such countries as Canada, the United States, Japan, Australia, and New Zealand. Along with numerous diocesan priests and men who belonged to religious communities, the Irish Sisters of Charity, Marist Sisters, Presentation Sisters, Religious of the Sacred Heart, Sisters of Mercy, and many other nuns founded schools, colleges, and hospitals around the world. They came from France, Germany, Ireland, Italy, and other European countries. The missionary activity of Nano Nagle (1718–84), St Rose Philippine Duchesne (1769–1852), Catherine Elizabeth McAuley (1778–1841), Mary Aikenhead (1787–1858), St Jeanne Jugan (1792–1879), St Francis Xavier Cabrini (1850–1917), and their associates played a key role in creating world Catholicism. But this expansion of European Catholicism had hardly started before divisions arose at home—with the 16th-century Protestant Reformation.

The Reformation

At least since the Council of Vienne (1311–12), a cry for 'reform in head and members' was heard in the Catholic Church, since her life at various levels had become marked by many grave abuses. The situation was aggravated by the long absence from the diocese of Rome when the popes lived in Avignon (1309–77); by the Great Western Schism (1378–1417), a period when eight popes and antipopes (those claiming to be bishop of Rome in opposition to those lawfully elected) divided Western Christianity; and by the Black Death, or bubonic plague, which suddenly arrived in 1346 and killed up to twenty million people, at least one-quarter of the European population. Europe did not reach its pre-plague level again until the 16th century began. The most generous priests, monks, and friars suffered disproportionately, since they risked infection by helping the sick and dying. This loss of the best religious leadership played its part in demoralizing the Church and society. The scandalous lives of such Renaissance popes as Alexander VI, who secured his own election largely through bribes and devoted much of his papal energies to furthering the position of his children, made reformation a crying need.

Judgements over the health or sickness of the Catholic Church in different countries still vary greatly. What, for example, was the situation like in England on the eve of the Reformation? Was the official Church there meeting the spiritual needs of ordinary people? Eamon Duffy and others have challenged the conventional picture of a dysfunctional Catholicism in radical need of reform. But the debate still continues about the state of English faith before Henry VIII (king of England 1509–47) broke with the papacy and seized the monasteries and their property. The vigour of 16th-century Catholicism in Spain has come to be more widely recognized. Cardinal Ximenez de Cisneros (d. 1517) reformed the religious orders and encouraged the new learning. Among other contributions, he commissioned the first polyglot Bible of modern times, a six-volume work with parallel texts in Hebrew, Greek, and Latin. The monarchy controlled ecclesiastical affairs, insisted on religious-political orthodoxy, and helped make Spain an intensely Catholic society. Scholarship flourished, with Dominican theologians and philosophers leading the way. One of them, Francisco de Vitoria (d. 1546), developed a theory of international law that has proved lastingly important. Dominicans, Franciscans, and Jesuits provided an army of missionaries for evangelizing the New World. Mystics, such as St John of the Cross (d. 1591), St Teresa of Avila (d. 1582), and St Ignatius Loyola (d. 1556), left their mark on the whole Christian world through their lives and writing.

In the Low Countries, Erasmus of Rotterdam (d. 1536), through his *Praise of Folly* (1509), satirized the scandalous abuses he witnessed in monasteries and the Church at large. But Thomas à Kempis (d. 1471) had lived in the same part of Europe and composed the extraordinarily popular *Imitation of Christ*, a text that described for all ages what a life centred on Jesus involves.

The start of the Protestant Reformation, often simply and better called the Reformation, is traditionally dated to 1517 when Martin Luther (1483–1546) produced his ninety-five theses in protest against the scandalous sale of indulgences and other abuses of papal and clerical power. The official Church granted 'indulgences', or remissions of punishment in purgatory, for sinners who had repented of their sins but had died without making full satisfaction for the harm they had caused. On the authority of Pope Leo X, indulgences were being sold to raise money from the German faithful to help pay for building the new St Peter's Basilica in Rome. Luther felt outraged not only at this squalid practice but also at the whole idea that Church leaders could exercise control over the fate of human beings in the afterlife.

Intensely concerned with being justified by Christ ('Where do I find a gracious God who will heal the wounds of my guilt-stricken conscience?'), Luther argued for justification through divine grace alone (*sola gratia*), by faith alone (*sola fide*), and not by good works. He understood the Bible, and not human traditions, to be the only authoritative rule for faith (*sola scriptura*), and spread knowledge of the scriptures by translating the Bible into German. He also introduced the vernacular for the celebration of the Eucharist, demanded that lay people should receive Communion 'under both kinds' (that is, both the consecrated bread *and* wine), defended the right of clergy to marry, and opposed the authority of the pope.

Among the plethora of Protestant groups that emerged at the Reformation, some were extreme, even anarchical, but others were committed to clear ideas and precise ecclesiastical order. Jean Calvin (1509–64) promoted this style of Reformation in France, Switzerland, and elsewhere. In his commentaries on the scriptures and his *Institutes* (first edition 1536), he showed himself a more rigorous theologian than Luther and more aware of the importance of organization. Presbyterianism, the form of

Church government created by Calvin, involves rule through a series of courts, up to the General Assembly—with the representative ministers and elders being elected.

Undoubtedly, nationalism and economic interests helped the cause of the Reformation. But it was a deeply felt religious movement that aimed to purify Church life and base Christian existence on the scriptures. Luther and Calvin expressed complementary emphases of perennial theological importance. Where Luther's call for reform was more oriented towards human beings who hear and believe the word of God, Calvin highlighted the majesty of God who elects the predestined and gives them the grace of obedient faith. In the 20th century, the Second Vatican Council (1962–5) was to acknowledge frankly 'that continued reformation' to which Christ always calls his Church (*Unitatis Redintegratio*, 6)—a confession that converged with the Reformers' sense of the enduring power of sin that threatens communion with God.

Nevertheless, despite appropriate respect for Calvin, Luther, and other leading Reformers, Catholics drew some lines: for instance, against Luther's notion of the human will being simply 'captive' to evil. Erasmus in *On Free Will* (1524), while respecting the sovereignty of God's grace and action, defended the free will of human beings. Erasmus' edition of the New Testament in Greek (1516) proved not only a landmark for biblical scholarship but also expressed his desire to reform Christian life in the light of the scriptures. But like the Catholic bishops at the reforming Council of Trent (1545–63), Erasmus maintained that human beings freely responded to God's gifts. He opposed division in Christendom as the price of badly needed reform.

Meeting over three periods for a total of eighteen years, the Council of Trent remains the longest council in the history of the Catholic Church. Held in the northern Italian city of Trent, it was the culmination of a movement for Catholic renewal that pre-dated Luther. The first eight sessions (1545–7) did, however, treat such major themes raised by the Reformers as the relationship between scripture and tradition, justification, original sin, and the sacraments. Tensions between Emperor Charles V and the pope led to a suspension of the Council, which eventually resumed for a second period (1551–2). The achievements of sessions nine to fourteen included decrees on the Eucharist and on the sacraments of penance (now called reconciliation) and extreme unction (now called anointing of the sick). After the new French king, Henry II, joined forces with some German princes who defeated Charles V and even threatened to overrun Trent, the Council was once again adjourned; it finally met again for a third period (1562–3). Its sessions fifteen to twenty-five defined doctrines about the Eucharist, the sacraments of orders and matrimony, and purgatory or purification after death from the effects of sin.

Trent brought more uniformity to Western or Latin Catholicism, with the standard Missal for Mass, the standard breviary (or book for daily prayer by priests and others), the Roman Catechism of 1566 (the first catechism published in the aftermath of any council), and the Sixto-Clementine Bible of 1592, the standard (Latin) text of the scriptures. Through restating and/or reforming many beliefs and practices, the Council of Trent reshaped Catholicism down to the 20th century.

The Council led to the founding of seminaries, special colleges for the spiritual, intellectual, and pastoral training of candidates for the priesthood. St Charles Borromeo (1538–84), the influential archbishop of Milan, backed the foundation of seminaries. He encouraged the installation of altar rails in churches, which visibly expressed a division between the ordained priest who celebrated the Mass in the sanctuary and the baptized faithful who attended public worship in the nave, or central part of the church. Only a few churches built in earlier centuries had featured pulpits. New churches now regularly included prominent pulpits from which priests and bishops proclaimed Catholic doctrine. Religious orders sprang up and, through preaching, spiritual direction, and other ministries, aimed to renew Christian life. After being founded in 1540, the Jesuits quickly turned to education to spread faith and further the reformation of Christendom. By establishing colleges in many countries, they became known as 'the schoolmasters' of Europe and the New World.

Trent sealed a parting of the ways between Catholics and Protestants. In a prophetic mode, Protestants had denounced the worldliness and corruption of Catholicism and rightly championed the scriptures as the sacred norm for Christian life. But they reduced the sacramental mediation of God's grace to baptism and the Eucharist. By maintaining the seven sacraments (baptism, confirmation, the Eucharist, penance or reconciliation of sinners, anointing of the sick, holy orders, and matrimony), the Catholic Church maintained a tradition that blessed all dimensions of human life. In the 18th century, Dr Samuel Johnson (1709–84) expressed this difference. Old, ill, and saddened by the thought of dying, he declared in the last summer of his life:

> A good man of a timorous disposition, in great doubt of his acceptance with God, and pretty credulous, may be glad of a church where there are so many helps to get to heaven. I would be a Papist, if I could. I have fear enough, but an obstinate rationality prevents me.

Even before the Council of Trent closed in 1563, the religious map of Europe was being redrawn. When Elizabeth I succeeded to the throne in 1558, England definitively ceased to be in communion with the bishop of Rome. The Church of England became an attractive third choice, alongside Catholicism and Protestantism.

Under the leadership of bishops in communion with the archbishop of Canterbury, Anglicanism understood itself to maintain the mainstream tradition of early Christianity, to be faithful to the scriptures, and to provide a middle road between papal authority and Protestant reform.

Jesuits became deeply involved in the struggle to save Austria, England, Germany, Poland, Scotland, and other countries for the one Catholic Church. But before the 16th century ended, not only England, Scotland, and Wales, but also parts of Germany and the Low Countries, Scandinavia, and some cantons of Switzerland had broken away from Catholicism. The political dimension of religious differences culminated in the Thirty Years War (1618–48), which weakened Spain, strengthened France, and devastated Germany. Hostilities ended in 1648 with two treaties forming the Peace of Westphalia; it endorsed the principle of 'cuius regio eius religio', roughly translated as 'the government of a state determines its religious adherence'. This peace settlement extended protection to most religious minorities (whether Protestants in Catholic states or vice versa). Innocent X (pope 1644–55) denounced the treaties of Westphalia in a papal bull, but was universally ignored.

The new learning

Just as reform movements pre-dated Luther's protests, so too did the growth of new learning and thinking. Fifteenth-century Florence, universities across Europe, religious orders, rulers, and other individuals such as Johannes Gutenberg (d. 1468) fostered a new literacy and learning that shaped the world in which Catholics lived and thought. In the 2nd century AD, printing had begun in China, but geographical separation and, later, the opposition of Islam prevented this development from reaching Europe. In 1450, Gutenberg, a Mainz blacksmith, created a movable typeface of identical letters and invented what we know as the printing press. A vast reading public grew up; mass literacy was on the way. Gutenberg made possible the new humanism of such figures as Erasmus, his friends Thomas More (d. 1535) and John Colet (d. 1519) in England, and Charitas Pirckheimer

(d. 1532) in Nuremberg. Benedictines, Dominicans, and other religious orders, both old and new, spread literacy and learning.

In the post-Gutenberg world, Catholics and others had many things to learn and to question. The new learning, no less than the discovery of other continents and the Reformation, challenged old certainties. Was monarchy God's chosen form of government, so that it would always be sinful to rebel against a monarch? Or could one agree with the Jesuit Juan Mariana (1536–1624) and justify in certain circumstances killing a tyrant? Was St Robert Bellarmine (1542–1621) correct in opposing the 'divine right of kings' and in holding that popes enjoyed only indirect, not direct, power in temporal matters? Could and should the state be used to enforce Church requirements?

More than a century later, over in North America, Charles Carroll (1737–1832) became the only Catholic among fifty-five signatories of the American Declaration of Independence (1776). During the colonial era, Catholics had been almost everywhere a victimized minority. Along with his cousin, Archbishop John Carroll of Baltimore (1736–1815), who was the first Catholic bishop in the United States and the founder of Georgetown University (Washington, DC), Charles Carroll symbolized American religious freedom and a sense that the Catholic faith could and should be reconciled with the best features of the new, democratic political order.

The European union of altar and throne, which reached back to Emperor Constantine and was widely considered the norm for Catholic life, came to a grinding halt when the furies raged in the French Revolution. The Reign of Terror (1793–4) targeted clergy and religious men and women along with aristocrats, while the revolutionary government slaughtered devout peasants in the Vendée. When Napoleon had Pius VI (pope 1775–99) carried off as a prisoner to France, he took the Catholic Church to the edge. The troubles of the French Revolution unhinged papal power and prestige, and reduced the Catholic Church in France to its weakest state for over a thousand years.

But in post-Napoleonic France and beyond, Catholicism enjoyed a dramatic resurgence. New religious congregations of men and women, often with a missionary commitment, sprang up. Old and new devotions flowered: such as veneration of the Sacred Heart of Jesus and the use of the 'miraculous medal' which carried the image of the Virgin Mary. After the 1858 visions of St Bernadette Soubirous (1844–79), Lourdes became a place of pilgrimage for millions. Blessed Frédéric Ozanam (1813–53) founded in 1833 the Society of St Vincent de Paul, which continues to serve poor people.

Catholic teaching and scholarly life remained, however, at a low level. Before and after Napoleon, Catholics and other Christians faced a serious challenge from the Enlightenment, the first major intellectual movement in the Western world for well over a thousand years to develop outside the control of the Catholic Church. Started in 17th-century Europe and then spread to the Americas, it resisted authority and tradition, championed human rights, encouraged empirical methods in scientific research, and aimed at deciding issues through the use of reason alone. Many personages of the Enlightenment rejected miracles and special divine revelation, and could be strongly opposed to official Christianity.

Some positive responses to the Enlightenment came from figures like Blessed John Henry Newman (1801–90) and the founder of modern Catholic biblical studies, the Dominican Marie-Joseph Lagrange (1855–1938). In a major document, the First Vatican Council (1869/70) defended a proper collaboration between faith (the response to divine revelation) and reason in all its forms. Leo XIII (pope 1878–1903) reacted to industrial urbanization and the social problems that ensued by defending the rights of workers in his encyclical of 1891, *Rerum Novarum* ('of new things'). He drew on a German pioneer of Catholic social teaching, Bishop William Emmanuel von Ketteler (1811–77), and found much support from Cardinal Henry Edward Manning (1808–92), who dedicated himself to improving social conditions for workers in England and Ireland. An Austrian abbot, Johann Gregor Mendel (1822–84), through his experiments with peas in the monastery garden, demonstrated the primary source of variability in plants and animals and became the father of modern genetics.

But, in general, reactionary and closed attitudes prevailed well into the 20th century. Despite some attractive features of his papacy, Blessed Pius IX (pope 1846–78) epitomizes this resistance. In the eighty propositions of his *Syllabus of Errors* (1864), he published a comprehensive attack on 'modern errors'. Besides condemning views that most Christians would reject (such as 'any action of God on human beings and the world must be denied', and 'faith in Christ is detrimental to human reason'), he also reasserted the temporal power of popes and opposed freedom of speech and religion. He used public executions in an attempt to maintain civil order right up to 1870, when the papal states fell and the forces of united Italy entered Rome. Although the 19th century saw the emancipation of Jews in most countries, in 1850 Pius IX reinstated in the city a closed ghetto for Jews and introduced anti-Jewish legislation. At a time when slavery was being abolished, he argued that it could be reconciled with divine revelation and the natural law.

Pius IX died in 1878, exactly one century before the election of John Paul II, a pope who rejected the death penalty, repeatedly asked pardon for the wrongs Catholics have committed against Jews, and worked hard to further dialogue between the Catholic Church and other Christian bodies. During the pontificate of Pio Nono, John Paul II would have been gaoled in Castel San Angelo for saying, writing, and doing such things. At the end of the 20th century, his international impact depended in part on something

Pius IX could not imagine: namely, freedom from the burden and limitation of governing a sovereign country, the papal states.

The end of Pius IX's long pontificate witnessed struggles with hostile states: for instance, in Germany the anti-Catholic campaign led by Otto von Bismarck that reached its height in 1871–5, and the pressure on the Church from anticlerical governments in France after 1870. Such Church–state conflicts grew more violent in the 20th century: the killing of almost 7,000 priests and the destruction of hundreds of churches during the Spanish Civil War (1936–9), which ended with General Franco's ruthless suppression of his opponents; the persecution of many Catholics and other Christians in Nazi Germany (1933–45), along with the complicity of many Catholics and other Christians in Hitler's crimes; persecutions, under European Communism (down to 1989) and under Chinese Communism (since 1949); and endemic violence and oppression in some Muslim-dominated states.

The coming of the world Church

How can we sum up the situation of Catholicism at the end of the 20th century, one marked by the murderous catastrophes of two world wars? It proved a bloodstained century, with fifty-five million being killed or starving to death during the Second World War (1939–45) alone.

One act of wilful murder stands out: the Shoah. Adolf Hitler and his collaborators systematically exterminated nearly six million European Jews. After Rolf Hochhuth attacked Pius XII (pope 1939–58) in a play *The Deputy: A Christian Tragedy* (1963), it became popular to accuse Pius XII of failure to challenge the Nazis publicly over their dreadful murder of Jews. Books and articles have poured out, with the grounds for attack shifting over the years from 'he was indifferent to Jewish suffering in the Holocaust' (Hochhuth) to 'he was not as concerned about Nazi efforts to exterminate Jews as he should have been' (John

Cornwell in *Hitler's Pope* (1999)). In contrast, numerous writers have defended and praised Pius XII for all that he did to save Jews. They include such figures as an Anglican historian, Owen Chadwick, who established that Pius XII was party to a plot against Hitler in the winter of 1939/40, and a Jewish professor of history and political science, David G. Dalin, whose 2005 study answers the case brought by Cornwell and others. Without having done the historical research necessary to adjudicate the debate competently, I should mention that, when the Second World War ended, the chief rabbi of Rome became a Catholic and was baptized as 'Eugenio', the baptismal name of Pius XII. Eugenio Zolli then lived at the Gregorian University where I later lived (1974–2006).

Along with Nazism, the Communism of Joseph Stalin (1879–1953) and of Mao Tse-tung (1893–1976) marked the century until, at least in Europe, this ideology officially ended when the Berlin Wall came down in November 1989. The sudden collapse of the Soviet Union was perhaps the most surprising event in the entire century.

These and other changes affected the 20th-century story of Catholicism. In 1900, almost two-thirds of the world's Catholics lived in Europe and North America; by 1993, three-quarters of them lived in Latin America, Africa, and Asia. In an even more startling demographic change, when the world population passed the six billion mark in October 1999, more than half the Catholics who have ever existed lived in the 20th century.

Another way of expressing the shift is to recall the conclave of cardinals who elected Paul VI (pope 1963–78); 65 per cent of those cardinals were Europeans and more than one-third were Italians. By the time of the 1978 conclave that elected John Paul II, the Italian cardinals were down to one-quarter and those from Western Europe down to fewer than half. Beyond question, the Italians and Europeans were still over-represented in 1978, but a clear demographic change had come in the college of cardinals, and it was no accident that by electing John Paul II, they chose the first non-Italian pope in more than 400 years.

John Paul II as a Polish bishop had attended Vatican II, the first Ecumenical Council to show the universality of the Catholic Church. Even so, the Council manifested a trend rather than an achieved reality. For example, only 311 of around 2,600 Council Fathers came from Africa; of these 311, only 60 were Africans. Nevertheless, the Council showed how, within the Catholic Church and beyond, the old days of European hegemony were drawing to a close.

When the Council opened in October 1962, the Cuban Missile Crisis had brought the USA and the Soviet Union to the brink of a nuclear war. John XXIII (pope 1958–63), who had already called the Council, played a key role in defusing that crisis. A few months later, he published his plea for a new world order, *Pacem in Terris* ('Peace on Earth'). When he died in June 1963, some units of the Russian navy flew their flags at half-mast. In October 1965, a few weeks after the fourth session of Vatican II opened, Paul VI went to New York and addressed a message of peace ('Never again war') to the United Nations—being the first pope ever to speak to that body which represents the nations of the world (Figure 4).

Vatican II had a double aim: an *aggiornamento* (updating) of the Church's life, worship, and teaching; and new relationships with other Christians, as well as with Jews, Muslims, and members of other world religions. The first and last of the documents issued by the Council express the double aim. Through *Sacrosanctum Concilium* (4 December 1963), the bishops endorsed the reform of Catholic worship by, first, a return to earlier and simpler forms, and secondly, the use of the vernacular or local language. The last and longest conciliar text, *Gaudium et Spes* (7 December 1965), spelled out the bishops' ideals and values for Christian and human life. On the same day, Paul VI and the Orthodox Patriarch

4. Pope Paul VI and Dr Michael Ramsey, the Archbishop of Canterbury, in March 1966 sign a common declaration, which inaugurated an Anglican–Roman Catholic dialogue that they hoped would lead to unity in truth and faith.

of Constantinople issued a joint declaration, expressing their regret for nine centuries of division and hopes for future reconciliation. Through ceremonies held simultaneously in the Vatican and at the Patriarch's residence in Istanbul, they lifted the mutual excommunications between the Orthodox and the Catholic Churches.

The Council has affected the lives of Catholics in many ways: through the new rites for the administration of baptism and other sacraments; through closer relations with other Christians, Jews, and followers of different religions; through encouragement given to new forms of life consecrated to prayer and apostolic activity; through changes in the training of candidates for the ordained ministry; and through other smaller and larger changes. Many of the new directions are reflected in the 1983 Code of Canon Law (for the Western Church) and the 1990 Code of Canons of the

Oriental Churches (for the Eastern Church). The Council also opened the way for developments on a scale scarcely imaginable to earlier Catholics. Let me mention a few examples.

First, the papacy. Continuing and enormously expanding the travels of Paul VI, John Paul II (d. 2005) made the papacy a world presence by leaving Italy and visiting 129 nations in all five continents. He proved a global evangelist. Second, since Vatican II closed in 1965, the Church has experienced the rise of Catholic feminism, the work of liberation theologians (who frequently looked back to Las Casas for their inspiration), and fresh attempts at dialogue with world religions.

From the 1980s, revelations emerged about sexual abuse of minors committed by priests and male religious figures. What came all too slowly was justice and pastoral care for the victims (who have often endured profound suffering and incurred permanent psychological damage), along with the swift removal of perpetrators from ministerial work, and their being held accountable. A 'sick' clerical culture and secretive legal provisions, which cried out for reform, protected the perpetrators. Clericalism and Church law had allowed much abuse to continue and led bishops to practise cover-ups. The tragic scandal reached to the very top, with John Paul II refusing to face the evidence that established the sexual crimes committed over many years by Fr Marcial Maciel Degollado, the founder of the Legionaries of Christ.

After being elected pope in April 2005, Benedict XVI acted quickly to bring Fr Maciel to justice and encourage long-needed reforms, including clear apologies made to victims of sexual abuse in Australia and the United States. Yet his papacy often proved disappointing. An unfortunate remark he quoted about Muhammad during an address in Regensburg (12 September 2006) provoked angry reactions from Muslims. He spent too much time criticizing the moral relativism of Western countries, reintroduced traditional papal dress, imposed on English-speaking countries around the world an unfortunate, clumsy translation—or should one say 'transliteralization?'—of the Missal of Paul VI, and encouraged a return to the pre-Vatican II Latin Mass (often wrongly called 'the Tridentine Mass'). He gave high priority to bringing back into Catholic unity a tiny schismatic group (the Society of St Pius X) created by Archbishop Marcel Lefebvre, an arch-traditionalist who had attended Vatican II but never accepted its reforms. The archbishop illicitly ordained several bishops, including Richard Williamson, whose 'revisionist' views of history extended to Holocaust denial. Even though the conditions for doing so were not fulfilled, Pope Benedict lifted the excommunication incurred by Williamson at his episcopal ordination. In a very real sense, the pope redeemed much of his record through a humble decision to resign in February 2013.

Elected pope on 13 March 2013, Cardinal Jorge Bergoglio, the first Latin American pope, quickly showed a firm resolve to reform the Roman Curia and the Vatican Bank (officially called 'the Institute of Religious Works'). Rewards and cronyism have plagued the selection in Rome of bishops for dioceses around the world. Pope Francis himself provides an image for the new breed of pastoral bishops that he longs to introduce. He has also set himself to decentralize the administration of the Church and implement the Vatican II teaching on 'collegiality' or the co-responsibility of all bishops in leading the universal Church.

Karl Rahner (d. 1984), one of the greatest theologians of the 20th century, famously interpreted the Second Vatican Council as the coming of 'the global Church'. But much remains to make that truly happen. When Pope Francis created his first batch of new cardinals on 22 February 2014, nine of the sixteen under 80 years of age (and so eligible to vote at a papal election) were from Latin America and Asia. Europe and North America still made up over

60 per cent of the papal electors. Nevertheless, Francis took a step in the right direction. The composition of the cabinet of eight (now nine) cardinals that he established in April 2013 had already revealed his global, collegial intentions: the eight came from Africa, the Americas, Asia, Europe, and Oceania.

Chapter 3
Catholics on God and the human condition

What are the beliefs about God and the human condition
that hold together the worldwide Catholic Church? Here, if
anywhere, our answers reflect much common ground shared
by Catholics and other Christians. All Christians endorse the
Nicene-Constantinopolitan Creed (of 381), which summarizes
faith in the tripersonal God, the incarnation of the Son of God,
and the human path through baptism and the forgiveness of
sins to life everlasting.

The Bible and its authority

From the time of Justin Martyr and Irenaeus of Lyons in the
2nd century, the whole Bible has always been acknowledged as the
primary way of knowing God. When Catholics express faith in
God, they mean the God of Abraham, Isaac, and Jacob, identified
as the Father of Our Lord Jesus Christ, and known to the wide
world through the outpouring of the Holy Spirit at the first
Pentecost. It is the self-disclosure of God that is the primary
theme of the Bible. To be sure, Catholics share the Old Testament
belief that God is also disclosed through the visible works of
Creation. In the words of a psalm, 'the heavens proclaim the glory
of God and the firmament shows forth the work of his hands'
(Ps. 19: 1). But in the special initiative of God conveyed through

the history of the Old Testament and New Testament, the veil has been lifted on God and the divine plan for human beings.

Vatican II's 1965 Constitution on Divine Revelation (*Dei Verbum*) understands this disclosure to be primarily God's self-revelation, which invites the personal response of faith, and to be secondarily the communication of truths about God and human beings that would otherwise remain unknown. Thus *Dei Verbum* recognizes revelation to be first the personal manifestation of the divine Mystery (upper case) and secondly the disclosure of the divine mysteries (lower case) that were previously hidden from human knowledge and understanding. In revelation we primarily meet God and not divinely authorized truths. This understanding of God's self-manifestation entails presenting human faith as a matter of a total human response to the divine revelation. Far from being predominantly, or even exclusively, the mind accepting revealed truths, faith is the 'obedient' response of the whole person—head, heart, and actions—with the help of the Holy Spirit, to the self-manifestation of God (*Dei Verbum*, 5).

The self-revelation of God changes and even transforms human beings who hear the divine word and let themselves be opened up to God's self-manifestation. The Old Testament prophets appreciated how the divine words, so far from being merely informative statements, powerfully bring about results. God's word is like rain that causes germination, 'giving seed to the sower and bread to the eater' (Isa. 55: 10). God's revelation and saving activity may be distinguishable but are never separable; they belong together as the two sides of the loving self-communication of God. When Christ 'completes and perfects' the divine self-manifestation, he reveals that 'God is with us to liberate us from the darkness of sin and death and raise us up to eternal life' (*Dei Verbum*, 4). In the language of John's Gospel, Christ is the saving 'Life' of the world because he is the revealing 'Light' of the world, and vice versa.

Vatican II presents revelation as utterly centred on Christ. In his incarnation, life, death, resurrection, and co-sending (with God the Father) of the Holy Spirit, Christ forms the climax of the divine self-revelation (*Dei Verbum*, 4, 17). As John's Gospel puts it, 'the Word became flesh and lived among us, and we have seen his glory, the glory of the Father's only Son. It is God the only Son, who is close to the Father's heart, who has made him known' (John 1: 14, 18).

In one sense, the Christ-event was and remains the fullness and completion of divine revelation. Having spoken and acted through the visible presence of his incarnate Son and the sending of the Spirit, God has nothing greater to say, nothing more to reveal, and no other agent of revelation who could match Christ. In that sense, the historical revelation through Christ is full, unparalleled, and unsurpassable in principle. God can and will call up subordinate mediators of revelation, but they cannot be like Christ, either in kind or in degree. His divine identity puts him qualitatively beyond any possible 'rival' in the work of revelation (and salvation).

But in another sense, we do not yet enjoy the fullness and completion of revelation. The final vision of God is still to come. As St John puts it, 'Beloved, we are God's children now; what we will be has not yet been revealed. What we know is this: when he [God] is revealed, we will be like him, for we will see him as he is' (1 John 3: 2). As we wait in hope for this complete, saving revelation, we see and know only 'dimly' and not yet fully. Referring to the imperfect mirrors of his time, St Paul writes: 'Now we see in a mirror dimly, but then face to face. Now I know in part; then I shall understand fully, even as I have been fully understood' (1 Cor. 13: 12). Calling on the Letter to Titus 2: 13, Vatican II teaches that the 'glorious manifestation of our Lord, Jesus Christ' is still to come (*Dei Verbum*, 4). The 'not yet' of this future manifestation qualifies the revelation 'already' brought by Christ and the Holy Spirit.

Besides the past and future aspects of revelation, *Dei Verbum* also portrays revelation as an ongoing reality which is ever being actualized and constantly invites human faith: 'The "obedience of faith" (Rom. 16: 26) . . . must be given to the God who reveals' (no. 5). People are called, in one generation after another, to accept in faith the divine self-manifestation that was completed with Jesus and his first disciples. *Dei Verbum* associates revelation as it happened *then* with revelation as it happens *now* in the Church: 'God, who spoke in the past, continues to converse with the spouse of his beloved Son' (no. 8). Vatican II's Constitution on the Sacred Liturgy (*Sacrosanctum Concilium*), when expounding the various ways Christ is present in the Church's public worship, acknowledges that 'it is he himself who speaks when the sacred scriptures are read in church'; in the context of worship, 'Christ is still proclaiming his gospel' (nos. 7, 33). Just as faith is a present event, so too is the light of divine self-revelation that comes through the sacraments, preaching, reading the scriptures, public and private prayer, and many other channels that summon forth faith.

In short, Catholic teaching portrays the revelation of God not only as reaching its unsurpassable climax in the past (with Jesus Christ) but also as a present and future event. We can express this triple time reference by distinguishing between the climax of 'foundational' revelation (which took place back in the 1st century AD), 'dependent' revelation (which is ceaselessly actualized now for those who hear God's revealing word), and 'final' revelation (which will be the definitive self-revelation of God at the end of history).

After its opening chapter on divine revelation, *Dei Verbum* moves in its second chapter to the question of *tradition*, understood to be both the process of 'handing on' (tradition as act) and the living heritage that is handed on (tradition as content). Both the process and the heritage are located within the believing community. The dynamic of tradition was already at work when the Jewish people handed on the memory of their sufferings and the powerful disclosure of God, who delivered them from slavery in Egypt and brought them home from exile in Babylon. Parents passed on to their children the marvellous story of the saving acts of God (Deut. 6: 20–5; 26: 5–10). Tradition was the setting for appropriating the revelation of God in their history.

With the outpouring of the Holy Spirit, the whole Church was empowered to transmit her memory of the normative self-revelation of God that was completed with Christ and the New Testament community. Thus tradition involves the 'Church in her doctrine, life, and worship' transmitting to every generation 'all that she is, all that she believes' (*Dei Verbum*, 8). What then is the relationship between the inspired scriptures and the 'prior' and 'larger' realities of divine revelation and the Church in her 'transmitting' role?

As such, the scriptures are written testimonies which, after the history of divine revelation had begun, came into existence under the inspiration of the Holy Spirit and through the work of some believers at various stages in the foundational history of God's people. Thus the scriptures differ from revelation in the way that written texts differ from living, interpersonal events. It makes perfectly good sense to say with exasperation: 'I left my copy of the Bible behind in the London Underground.' But I would have a good deal of explaining to do if I were to say to a friend, 'I left revelation behind in the Underground.'

As an inspired text, the Bible illuminates the deepest reality of God and human beings; it is indispensable for Christian existence, both collectively and individually. Nevertheless, revelation or the living word of God remains a broader reality and is not limited to the Bible and its immediate impact. God's living word is not confined to a written text, even one written under the special guidance of the Holy Spirit.

Eventually, the inspired books were acknowledged for their unique authority and formed the *canon* of scripture, a closed list of texts that is normative for Catholic life and practice. A 1546 decree from the Council of Trent definitively established the biblical canon for Catholics. But the process of 'canonization' had begun in the early centuries of Christianity. Irenaeus upheld, on the one hand, the unique value of the New Testament scriptures, especially the Gospels according to Matthew, Mark, Luke, and John, against Gnostic attempts to add further 'gospels' and other texts. On the other hand, he defended the enduring authority of the Old Testament scriptures against Marcion's total rejection of them.

Concretely what are the canonical books of the Catholic Bible? *The Oxford Annotated Bible* prints first thirty-nine books of the Old Testament, then seven books (plus sections of books) under the heading of 'Apocryphal/Deuterocanonical' books (books composed or translated into Greek some time after 200 BC), and at the end the twenty-seven books of the New Testament. 'Deuterocanonical' is the Catholic name for those seven books (Tobit, Judith, Wisdom, Sirach or Ecclesiasticus, Baruch, and 1 and 2 Maccabees), plus further portions of other books, found in the Greek or Septuagint version of the Old Testament but not in the canon of Hebrew scriptures that emerged in the 2nd century AD. Protestants have normally called these writings 'Apocrypha' ('hidden' or 'not genuine') and have often excluded them from their Bibles. When Catholics and Orthodox believers speak of the 'deuterocanonical' ('of the second canon') books of the Bible, they do not intend a negative judgement, as if these books were less important or less inspired. The term refers rather to a delay in their securing a permanent place in the canon. 'Deuterocanonical' also suggests that the books in question were composed (or translated into Greek) at the end of the Old Testament period: that is to say, after the composition of the other Old Testament books.

The tripersonal God

When asked 'What is God like?', Catholics, along with other Christians, point to the scriptures, both the Old Testament and the New Testament. The first disciples of Jesus and early Christians maintained their inherited Jewish faith in one God (monotheism), but did so in the light of the life, death, and resurrection of Jesus (together with the outpouring of the Holy Spirit). Without abandoning Jewish monotheism, they came to accept a 'differentiated' monotheism that maintained 'one God' but distinguished within the Godhead between Father, Son, and Holy Spirit, as we see in the baptismal formula at the end of Matthew's Gospel (Matt. 28: 19). Since the Trinitarian faith of early Christianity identified YHWH (or 'Yahweh', the God of Israel) as the Father of Our Lord Jesus Christ (Eph. 1: 3, 17), we need to recall the antecedent Jewish faith in God.

Jewish faith grew through personal and collective encounters with God: from such shadowy figures as Abraham, Sarah, Melchizedek, and others who belonged to the patriarchal period (that lasted down to around 1200 BC), who are gratefully remembered in the New Testament (e.g. Rom. 4: 1–25; Heb. 5–7), and two of whom (Abraham and Melchizedek) are recalled in the First Eucharistic Prayer (or ancient 'Roman Canon' of the Latin rite), right down to Mary, Joseph, Elizabeth, Zechariah, Simeon, and Anna—those holy men and women who people Luke's account of Jesus' conception and birth (Luke 1–2).

From these chapters of Luke's Gospel, Catholics and other Christians have drawn some very Jewish prayers that have constantly nourished their faith in God and vision of God: the *Magnificat* (from the words of Mary), the *Benedictus* (from Zechariah), the *Nunc Dimittis* (from Simeon)—not to mention the *Gloria in Excelsis Deo* inspired by the angelic praise when Christ was born (Luke 2: 14) and the *Ave Maria*, or *Hail Mary*, inspired by words addressed to Mary by the angel Gabriel and Elizabeth (Luke 1: 28, 42). To be sure, Catholic and Christian faith in God has been nourished even more by the Lord's Prayer (Matt. 6: 9–13). But the vision of God which Jesus conveyed in that prayer is, for the most part, deeply rooted in the Old Testament.

Dramatic moments punctuated the long Jewish experience of salvation history. God appeared to Moses in a 'flame of fire' that came out of a blazing bush in the wilderness, presenting himself as 'the God of Abraham, Isaac, and Jacob' and revealing the divine name of YHWH, interpreted as 'I am who I am' or 'I will be who I will be'. God commissioned Moses to liberate the chosen people from their captivity in Egypt (Exod. 3: 1–4: 17). Their deliverance involved not only forty years of wandering in the desert but also God's covenant at Mount Sinai, pre-eminent among the seven covenants gratefully recalled by Ben Sira (Sir. 44–7). From the outset, Christians understood the resurrection to embody and effect a new exodus from the slavery of sin and death, and the Eucharist to 're-present' the new covenant with God that Jesus instituted at the Last Supper.

Traditionally ascribed to King David, the psalms formed the hymnal of ancient Israel and were mostly composed to accompany acts of worship in the magnificent Temple constructed in Jerusalem by David's son and successor, King Solomon. The psalms reflected the people's personal experience of God, as they joyfully praised YHWH, asked for help in times of trouble, expressed confidence in the divine power, and, both collectively and individually, poured out their hearts to their God. The psalms became the prayerbook for Catholic Christianity, used day after day by communities and individuals in their public and private worship. For 2,000 years, the psalms have shaped and interpreted the sense that Catholics and other Christians have of who God is and what God does.

Catholics have learned more of God from using the psalms in prayer than from studying the teaching of general councils of the

Church. Philosophical thinking shaped this teaching, as when the Fourth Lateran Council (1215) confessed 'the one true God' to be 'eternal, immense [i.e. unmeasured and unmeasurable], unchangeable, incomprehensible, almighty, ineffable', and 'entirely simple'. The First Vatican Council (1869/70) added a few such attributes as God being 'infinite in intellect, will, and all perfection'. These precise adjectives can keep errors at bay. More importantly, the boundless attributes (God as in-finite, im-mense, and un-changeable, and therefore for us in-comprehensible and in-effable) respect the mysterious otherness of the divine Being who transcends human knowing. The central prayers of Catholic Christianity—the Lord's Prayer, the *Benedictus*, the *Magnificat*, the *Gloria in Excelsis Deo*—and the Nicene-Constantinopolitan Creed, have more to say about what God does (e.g. in creating all things, forgiving sins, and 'lifting up the lowly') than about what God is like (e.g. as sovereign Lord).

Their religious experience led the Israelites to develop an image of God that combined *majestic transcendence* and *loving closeness*. God was the utterly mysterious 'Other', three times acclaimed as holy by heavenly creatures (Isa. 6: 3). But God was also tenderly close to his people like a loving parent or spouse (e.g. Hos. 11: 3–4). Both this otherness and this closeness fed into the Catholic (and Christian) sense of God. On the one hand, as the *Sanctus* or *Trisagion*, the thrice holy acclaim of God passed into the worship of Catholics (and other Christians); in every Eucharistic prayer the *Sanctus* follows the preface. On the other hand, Jesus' sense of God being lovingly present as 'Abba', or 'Father dear', profoundly characterized his religious experience and preaching, and became the standard (but not exclusive) name for the first person of the divine Trinity.

It was Jesus who triggered the development from Jewish to Christian monotheism, or belief in one God now distinguished into *three persons*. At least implicitly, Jesus claimed an authority on a par with God. One can understand why some religious leaders rejected Jesus' claims as incompatible with their strict monotheism. After his resurrection from the dead, the earliest Christians proclaimed Jesus to be not just a wonderful human being vindicated by God but the only Son of God and their divine Lord.

In the opening greetings of his letters, St Paul set 'the Lord Jesus Christ' side by side with 'God our Father' as the source of 'grace and peace'—that is to say, of integral salvation. In a hymn that the apostle composed or, more likely, took over from early Christian worship (Phil. 2: 6–11), he attributed to Jesus 'equality with God', as well as the right to bear the divine name of 'Lord' and so receive adoration from the whole universe. A 'Trinitarian' farewell rounded off the apostle's Second Letter to the Corinthians: 'The grace of our Lord Jesus Christ and the love of God and the fellowship of the Holy Spirit be with you all' (2 Cor. 13: 13). Here 'the Lord Jesus Christ' was set alongside God (the Father) and the Holy Spirit.

After experiencing the risen Jesus, the first Christians and then Paul followed him in praying to God as 'Abba'. Paul and other New Testament Christians knew themselves to enjoy their adopted status as God's sons and daughters through receiving the Holy Spirit (Rom. 8: 14–17; Gal. 4: 4–7). Thus Christians, while maintaining faith in the one God (e.g. Gal. 3: 20), now included in their new form of monotheism Christ the Son of God and the Holy Spirit. They expressed this faith by baptizing 'in the name [singular] of the Father and of the Son and of the Holy Spirit' (Matt. 28: 19). This tripartite formula did not offer anything like the later doctrine of God as three in one and one in three. Admittedly, it implied a unity ('the name'), distinction, and equality between the Father, the Son, and the Holy Spirit. Yet the formula did not clarify such matters as their mutual relations. It provided, nevertheless, a starting point for confessing the Trinity and shaped profoundly Catholic worship.

Catholics (and many other Christians) invoke the Trinity when they sign themselves with the cross on their forehead, breast, and shoulders. The celebration of the Eucharist opens 'in the name of the Father, and of the Son, and of the Holy Spirit'; it closes with a blessing that calls on the Trinity. During the Eucharist, as well as in other liturgical ceremonies, the collects or variable prayers end by invoking the Trinity. In the divine office, the official prayer used by priests, religious, and many lay people, the canticles and psalms conclude with a doxology or praise of the Trinity: 'Glory be to the Father and to the Son and to the Holy Spirit, as it was in the beginning, is now, and ever shall be, world without end. Amen.' In the sacrament of penance, the priest pronounces words of absolution that are thoroughly Trinitarian:

> God, the Father of mercies, through the death and resurrection of his Son, has reconciled the world to himself and sent the Holy Spirit among us for the forgiveness of sins; through the ministry of the Church may God give you pardon and peace, and I absolve you from your sins in the name of the Father, and of the Son, and of the Holy Spirit.

For Catholics and other Christians, the 'law' of public worship has never ceased to indicate the central 'law' of belief: faith in the tripersonal God. Like Paul's teaching on Father, Son, and Holy Spirit, the liturgical usage remains firmly situated within the context of salvation and the experience of the baptized.

When encouraging Catholics to prepare for the Jubilee Year of 2000 and the coming third millennium, John Paul II swept aside suggestions about seven years of preparation, one for each of the seven sacraments. In his 1994 apostolic letter *Tertio Millennio Adveniente* ('As the third millennium approaches'), he went to the Trinitarian heart of the matter by inviting all Christians to dedicate in a special way 1997 to Jesus Christ, 1998 to the Holy Spirit, and 1999 to God the Father.

Those who wish to know what Catholics believe about the Trinity could well be advised to attend some church services, preferably in both the Eastern and Western rites. By listening carefully to the prayers and hymns, and by contemplating the icons and other images, they may appreciate what faith in the tripersonal God means in the great scheme of things to rank-and-file Catholic believers.

One could dedicate many more pages to other questions: about the Holy Spirit (such as the need for Western Catholics to develop a more vibrant sense of the Holy Spirit) and about Christ (in particular, an account of what is lost by those who deny his true divinity or reduce his full humanity). Limits of space require leaving all this to further reading.

Human beings: created, sinful, and redeemed

Catholics share with other Christians a faith in God, the 'Maker of all things, visible and invisible' (Nicene-Constantinopolitan Creed). Through creation, the sovereign divine freedom brought about a reality that differs from God and yet constantly and totally depends upon God. While always radically 'beyond' and 'other', God is so intimately present, especially to human beings, that St Augustine of Hippo could say to God in his *Confessions*: 'you were more inward than my inmost self'—or, as some translate these words, 'you were closer to me than I was to myself' (3.6).

God created man and woman in the divine image and likeness (Gen. 1: 26), so as to have, as Irenaeus put it, someone on whom to shower the divine gifts. In richly symbolic language, Genesis tells the story of the creation of 'Adam' and 'Eve' and their fall into sin. They transgressed the divine command, ate the forbidden fruit, and lost both their innocent relationship with each other and their trusting relationship with God. Far from enhancing their existence, sin left 'the man' and 'the woman' less than what they should have been and ushered in destructive consequences.

The most distressing consequence is death. Fashioned from dust (Gen. 2: 7), the man and the woman are by nature mortal. Their death should have been like that of Abraham, who was to die surrounded by his family in 'ripe old age'—a death that peacefully completed a life spent in faithful obedience to God (Gen. 25: 1–11). But disobedience to God has changed the experience of death for sinful human beings; death has become a troubling fate (Gen. 3: 19), a distressing sign of sin. Flanked by suffering and pain, death signals the radical change sin has brought to the human condition.

The opening chapters of Genesis present the sinfulness that emerged at humanity's origins as an enduring legacy of evil, which would be expressed in terms of inherited *original sin* and deliberate personal sin. For Pelagius (a scholar from the British Isles who came to Rome in the late 4th century) and his followers, the sin of Adam had not interiorly harmed his descendants and, in particular, had left quite intact the natural use of free will. Human beings can achieve salvation through their own sustained efforts. Augustine resisted the Pelagians on several grounds. First, the long-standing practice of baptizing infants, and doing so for the remission of sins, meant that infants come into the world with some kind of inherited sinful state. They are born deprived of the life of grace that they would have possessed but for Adam's sin. Second, since God sent his Son to save the whole of humanity, everyone must somehow be under the reign of sin and in need of Christ and baptism. Third, as a consequence of Adam's sin, the freedom of human beings remains deeply impaired, though not destroyed; we constantly need God's grace to share in the redemption brought by Christ. At no stage is salvation a 'do-it-yourself' affair.

The 16th-century leaders of the Protestant Reformation reopened the question of 'original sin', but at the other extreme from any Pelagian minimalizing of the damage caused by the fall of Adam and Eve. For Luther, Calvin, and others, the sin of our first parents totally corrupted human beings and destroyed their freedom.

Luther, in particular, identified human 'concupiscence', or disordered desire, as a direct consequence of Adam's fall and an irresistible inclination that persists even after baptism. In a decree on 'original sin' (1546), the Council of Trent accepted that concupiscence remains in the baptized but only as an 'inclination to sin', not 'sin in the true and proper sense'. The Council echoed the view of the *Exultet*, an ancient hymn of praise sung during the Easter Vigil, which, without using the term 'original sin', calls it 'the happy fault' that 'merited' for human beings such a Saviour.

Hence 'original sin' refers not only to human solidarity in sin but also to the call to a new, supernatural life in Christ. Far from being merely a depressing statement about the wounded nature of the inherited human condition, the doctrine of original sin underlines humanity's need for Christ's grace; there is no way to eternal life except through him.

In the primary and proper sense of the word, sin is always personal, a freely committed offence against a loving God for which the sinner must take responsibility and ask forgiveness. Sin means allowing oneself to become enslaved, corrupting one's human dignity and environment, and succumbing to an egotistical love of oneself, associated with a deep unwillingness to love God and one's fellow human beings. The salvation brought by Christ provides the remedy for this threefold evil of sin. He delivers sinners from the power of evil; he expiates or cleanses the defilement of sin; his love reconciles human beings to God and to one another.

Through the totally gratuitous gift of God, sinful human beings can enjoy the unmerited favour of being justified and saved in Christ through faith (Rom. 3: 24–5). They can be reborn (John 1: 13; 3: 3) and share in the new life of grace (Eph. 2: 4–6). This new life means becoming adopted children of God, brothers and sisters of the risen Christ, and 'temples' indwelt by the Holy Spirit (Rom. 8: 12–17; 1 Cor. 3: 16). This intimate sharing in the life of the Trinity (2 Pet. 1: 3–4) will be consummated beyond death through the immediate vision of God in the final kingdom. Thus the life of grace entails the hope of glory.

The Catholic *doctrine of grace* emerged from two great controversies. In the 4th and 5th centuries, the Pelagians stressed self-sufficient freedom, as if human beings were able to achieve salvation through their own resources. Against this, Augustine insisted that, from start to finish, human beings rely on God's loving grace if they are to be saved.

In the 16th century, the major Reformers held that human nature has been so deeply corrupted by 'original sin' that we remain steeped in sinfulness and commit sin in every action. Luther and Calvin used strong language about human depravity. But there is room for a generous reading of what the Reformers intended. The closer human beings draw to God in their spiritual lives, the more they will become aware of and even terrified by the overwhelming divine holiness that rises infinitely above our tainted and limited nature. Responding to the Reformers in 1547, the Council of Trent agreed on the utter primacy of divine grace in human justification and salvation. By their own free will, human beings cannot 'take one step towards justice in God's sight'. They must always be 'awakened and assisted by divine grace, if they are to repent of their sins and be reborn through baptism'. At the same time, the grace received in baptism interiorly transforms sinners. Through the strength constantly imparted by Christ, those who have been justified can and should perform good works that merit for them eternal life. They can freely cooperate with God's grace and do not necessarily 'sin in all their works'. What Trent taught here corresponds to a central conviction of Augustine: God crowns our merits, but, in doing so, he is in fact crowning his gifts.

Christ as fulfilment

The life of glory that the life of grace initiates is centred on the final coming of Christ in glory, the ultimate gift of God to human beings. Catholics have traditionally spoken of the 'last things', the first being death itself. A specifically Catholic understanding of death can be gleaned from the rites for the dying, from prayers written for Masses on behalf of the deceased, from burial rites, and from inscriptions on tombs. The conviction that 'life is changed, not taken away' characterizes this attitude towards death. Catholics (and other Christians) face death with a hope centred on the risen and living Christ. At funeral Masses, the presence of the great Easter candle near the coffin illustrates this hope. Christ, who has been the dead person's light and life since baptism, will continue to be that light now that the deceased is born into never-ending life.

With death, the history of each person assumes its complete, irreversible character, and is 'judged' by God in what came to be called the 'particular judgement'. At death, individuals know their condition in relationship with God. But are they all ready for the face-to-face vision of God that will bring them eternal happiness? Realizing that many deceased needed first to be cleansed (through Christ's merits) from the effects of their sins in a state that would be called 'purgatory', from early times Christians prayed to God for the dead and celebrated the Eucharist for them. On her deathbed, St Monica (d. 387) asked Augustine and her other son to 'remember her at the altar of God'.

After such post-mortem purification (or immediately, if this is not needed), those who die in the love of God are gifted with an immediate and eternal vision of the tripersonal God. They dwell with God and enjoy the utterly fulfilling vision of the infinitely good and beautiful God. As the 1992 *Catechism of the Catholic Church* puts it, there will be 'the blessed community of all who are perfectly incorporated in Christ' (no. 1026).

If such glory awaits the blessed in heaven, what of people who definitively close themselves to God's saving love? Hell (as a state of permanent and painful separation from God) remains a possibility for those who through deliberate malice refuse to love God and their neighbour (see Matt. 25: 31–46). With death their choice is sealed forever. But, as John Paul II taught (in 1999), one does not know 'whether or which human beings are found in hell'. Catholics (and other Christians) may and should pray that this terrible possibility will never be realized for anyone. Jesus warned about the possible outcome of serious sin. Yet Catholics may hope that the divine purpose to save everyone will be effective (1 Tim. 2: 3–6) and that, finally, God will be 'all in all' (1 Cor. 15: 28).

When Jesus comes in glory at the 'general judgement', the whole of humanity will definitively know the truth about itself. Through the resurrection of the dead, human beings will experience a gloriously transformed existence in 'the new heavens and the new earth' (2 Pet. 3: 13). Not only humanity but also the whole cosmos will be transfigured. In this ultimate union with Christ (John 14: 3), the earthly life of grace will pass over into the heavenly life of glory. The blessed will share in the ecstatic communion of mutual love that is the eternal life of the three divine persons.

Chapter 4
The sacraments and the Catholic Church

Presenting the sacraments before dealing with the Church may seem like putting the cart before the horse. But Catholic teaching did just that. Augustine and other fathers of the Church, the Council of Florence (1438–45), and the Council of Trent (1545–63) taught much about baptism, the Eucharist, and the other sacraments long before official teaching on the nature and functions of the Church took shape at the First Vatican Council (1869/70) and, above all, at the Second Vatican Council (1962–5).

For those who wish to know more about the sacraments, the short answer would be attendance at the Easter Vigil on Holy Saturday. There the Rite of Christian Initiation of Adults (the RCIA), introduced in 1972 as a result of Vatican II (*Sacrosanctum Concilium*, 64), reaches its climax and, after their long preparation, candidates are received into the Catholic Church through the sacraments of baptism, confirmation, and the Eucharist. The long answer is the first half of this chapter.

The seven sacraments

Unquestionably, the divine gifts are not limited to the seven sacraments of baptism, confirmation, Eucharist, penance, the anointing of the sick, holy orders, and matrimony. But they are seven central means for the common worship of God, privileged means that bring Catholics together in a community of mutual support and enable them to experience the risen Christ as effectively present in their lives. The sacraments are vivid, perceptible signs (that can be seen, heard, tasted, touched, and smelled); they create ritual dramas that take believers into a sacred time and place. They help participants to absorb the truths and values of Christian faith or allow such truths and values to revivify. The sacraments confer and strengthen the new life of grace in the particular form that each sacrament symbolizes.

The word 'sacrament' in Latin originally referred to oath-taking, consecration, or ritual obligation. It came to mean some ritual action that blesses human beings with the saving life communicated through Christ's life, death, and resurrection and the outpouring of the Holy Spirit.

Christian initiation

I begin with baptism, confirmation, and the Eucharist. Together, these three sacraments constitute full initiation into Catholic life. They mark a movement away from one kind of identity and status to another. The initiated 'die' to a former way of life and are 'resurrected' or 'reborn' to another. Christian initiation, or at least baptism, has been interpreted as a death, burial, and resurrection (Rom. 6: 1–14) and rebirth (John 3: 5; Titus 3: 5). The stages of Christian initiation include *separation*, or entrance into the catechumenate; *preparation* or transition, when catechumens are instructed in Christian teaching and life and learn to pray with the community; and *celebration* (baptism, confirmation, and First Communion) by which the catechumens 'put on' Christ (Gal. 3: 26–7) and are incorporated into the one body of the community (1 Cor. 12: 13).

From the start of Christianity, baptismal washing and initiation were understood to be one process of justification and sanctification, in which the tripersonal God remits sins and communicates new life, and in which human beings enter into the Body of Christ (1 Cor. 6: 11). Like the dying and rising of Christ himself, baptism has a once-and-for-all character; it can never be repeated.

In controversies that flared up in the 4th and 5th centuries over the worthiness or unworthiness of the one who administered baptism, St Augustine of Hippo clarified for all time that the validity and efficacy of the sacrament do not essentially depend upon the personal holiness of the minister. The invisible Christ, and not the visible minister, is the primary minister of baptism and of the other sacraments. As Augustine put it, Christ is actively present as the invisible minister of baptism, even if the sacrament were to be visibly administered by an arch-traitor like Judas Iscariot himself.

In the 14th and 15th centuries, the issue returned when John Wyclif and John Huss argued that sacraments administered by a sinful priest or bishop were not effective. In 1415, the Council of Constance insisted that even 'a bad priest' truly and validly administers the sacraments, provided he observes the essentials in performing the sacraments and 'has the intention of doing what the Church does'. The sinfulness of the minister (and/or the sinfulness of the recipient) may stop baptism (and other sacraments) from enjoying their full and fruitful effect. But it would create an intolerable uncertainty about such validity (and fruitfulness) if those receiving baptism or other sacraments had to be sure that the minister was personally in a state of grace and friendship with God. In his novel *The Power and the Glory*, Graham Greene (1904–91) followed Augustine: during a persecution in Mexico, people to whom a sinful priest ministered knew they received the sacraments validly and fruitfully.

Eastern Catholics and other Eastern Christians have maintained the ancient practice of the Church: even in the case of infants, baptism, confirmation, and Holy Communion are administered together. But in the West, an anointing after baptism, associated with the imposition of hands and an invocation of the Holy Spirit, developed into a separate rite. This was administered by the bishop, who as head of the local church *confirmed* what had been done in baptism and incorporated the baptized fully into the community. Confirmation was delayed for years, with First Communion coming earlier at the age of reason. Postponed until adolescence or early adulthood, confirmation became the sacrament of a mature faith commitment. Any sense of the unified process of Christian initiation was widely lost.

Vatican II wanted to retrieve a richer sense of what confirmation brings: through this sacrament the faithful 'are more perfectly bound to the Church' and 'are, as true witnesses of Christ, more strictly obliged to spread the faith by word and deed' (*Lumen Gentium*, 11). Already given in baptism, the Holy Spirit descends more fully on those being confirmed and draws them into the witness that the Spirit gives to the Father and the Son (Rom. 8: 16–17).

In an interconnected process of Christian initiation, baptism and confirmation reach their goal in the *Eucharist* (Greek for 'thanksgiving'). Unlike the other sacraments which were indirectly instituted by Christ, this sacrament comes directly from something that Jesus said and did at the end of his earthly life: the institution of the Eucharist during the Last Supper. Convergent New Testament traditions (from 1 Cor. 11: 23–6 and the Gospels) support this conclusion: at a sacrificial meal before he died, Jesus invited his disciples to share, by eating and drinking, in his covenant offering to the Father. Elements of the Passover liturgy/ meal were taken up and shaped the early Christian Eucharist, but it was very quickly celebrated every Sunday and not merely once a year (as in the case of the Jewish Passover). By the 3rd century, if not earlier, many Christians attended the Eucharist on a daily basis.

In this sacrifice of praise, thanksgiving, and expiation for sins, Christ functioned as both priest and victim. His priestly words and gestures (the breaking of the bread/body and the 'pouring out of my blood') were understood sacrificially. These words and actions symbolized and enacted a covenant of reconciliation that bound human beings in a new relationship with God and with one another. While the Last Supper formed a key element in his sacrifice, it was also a meal involving consecrated bread and wine: 'take and eat' and 'drink all of you' (Matt. 26: 26–7).

Out of its Jewish heritage, early Christianity developed a Liturgy of the Word to precede the Liturgy of the Eucharist. The former constitutes the first part of Mass, with opening prayers of praise and repentance, readings from the Bible (followed ideally by a homily), intercessions for the Church and the world, and (on important days) the Creed or confession of faith. Then follows the Liturgy of the Eucharist, with the preparation of the gifts, the *anamnesis*, *epiclesis*, and *doxology*, leading to the Lord's Prayer, a sign of reconciliation and peace, the reception of communion, and a final blessing. A single, integrated rite moves from word and worship to the Eucharistic meal. Several terms call for explanation.

The *anamnesis*, as remembering or recalling the past, involves bringing to mind the saving action of God in history, especially in the life, passion, death, resurrection, and glorification of Christ. As anticipation, *anamnesis* means looking forward to the final fulfilment and doing so with an expectation that already experiences something of that ultimate reality. Thus *anamnesis* entails memory, experience, and hope. St Paul incorporated these three elements into his account of the Eucharist: 'As often as you eat this bread and drink this cup, you proclaim [in the present] the death of the Lord [in the past] until he comes [in the future]' (1 Cor. 11: 26). The re-presentation here and now (in the shared eating, drinking, and 'proclaiming' of Christ's death and resurrection), the memorial of the foundational, once-and-for-all past event of salvation (the 'doing in remembrance' of Jesus who was handed over symbolically at the Last Supper and physically on Calvary), and the expectation of his coming (which makes the Eucharist an anticipation of the final kingdom) are woven together in the liturgy. More than a thousand years later, the Pauline theme of Eucharistic experience, memory, and hope was expressed in a text for the feast of Corpus Christi (the feast of 'the Body of Christ' instituted in 1264 to celebrate the gift of the Eucharist):

> O sacred banquet in which Christ is received: the memory of his suffering is recalled [past], (our) mind is filled with grace [present], and we receive a pledge of the glory that is to be ours [future].
> (O sacrum convivium, in quo Christus sumitur, recolitur memoria passionis eius; mens impletur gratia; et futurae gloriae nobis pignus datur.)

In the Eucharistic prayers, the *epiclesis*, or 'invocation', normally asks that the Holy Spirit descend upon the gifts of bread and wine to change them into the body and blood of Christ for the transformation of those who receive them. In the new Eucharistic prayers introduced after Vatican II, the *epiclesis before* the narrative of the institution of the Eucharist prays that the Spirit may descend upon the gifts to transform them, while the *epiclesis after* the institution narrative prays that the communicants may be changed. Thus in *epiclesis* the Spirit is invoked and actualizes the Eucharistic presence of Christ; in *anamnesis* Christ is remembered, experienced, and anticipated. Then the *doxology*, or 'giving glory to God', completes the Eucharistic prayer, by directing 'all glory and honour' to God the Father, 'through, with, and in' Christ 'in the unity' created by the Holy Spirit.

Right from the beginning, Christians appreciated four blessings effected by the Eucharist: the *unity* of believers, who shared in Christ's perfect *sacrifice*, experienced his special *presence* through the consecrated elements, and were prepared for a glorious *resurrection*. First, Paul insisted that sharing in the one Eucharistic bread and in the one cup meant belonging to the one Body of Christ (1 Cor. 10: 16–17). A 5th-century prayer (from the *Liturgy of St Basil*) expressed this desire for Catholic unity: 'May all of us who partake of the one bread and chalice be united to one another in the communion of the same Holy Spirit.' Second, right from the time of the *Didache* (a text written about AD 90), Christians invoked Malachi 1: 11 to interpret the Eucharist as the 'pure sacrifice for the nations'. Third, they commonly appealed to the miracle at Cana (John 2: 1–11) and affirmed a profound change in the Eucharistic elements. Thus St Cyril of Jerusalem (d. 386) reminded his hearers: 'In Cana of Galilee he [Christ] changed water into wine (and wine is akin to blood). Is it incredible that he should change wine into blood? . . . Therefore with complete assurance let us partake of these elements as being the body and blood of Christ' (*Mystagogic Catecheses*, 4. 2. 3). Fourth, St Irenaeus of Lyons (d. around 200) assured believers that by feeding 'on the flesh and blood of the Lord', their 'flesh' would enjoy the eternal life of resurrection (*Adversus Haereses*, 5. 2. 2–3).

In later centuries, two of these four blessings became controversial: the nature of the risen Christ's *presence* under the Eucharistic elements; and the *sacrificial character* of the Eucharist. From the 11th century, controversy emerged about the change in the Eucharistic elements and the nature of Christ's presence. A crudely realistic view of his presence and a purely symbolic version that excluded any real change in the elements marked the two extremes. Theologians and then official teaching began to apply 'transubstantiated' to what happens when the bread and wine become the body and blood of the risen Christ. The 'substance' of bread and wine is changed into Christ's body and blood, while the 'accidents', or secondary characteristics, of the elements remain. In the 16th century, Protestant Reformers raised again the issue of the Eucharistic presence. Some, like Ulrich Zwingli (1484–1531), maintained that the elements undergo no change whatsoever, and that the Lord's Supper is a memorial with a 'spiritual' and merely symbolic meaning.

Faced with such challenges, the Council of Trent in a decree of 1551 affirmed the doctrine of 'transubstantiation', distinguished between the 'substance' and the 'outward appearances' (*species*) of bread and wine, but refrained from employing the pair of terms 'substance' and 'accidents', which through the influence of Thomas Aquinas had become normal usage. After acknowledging that 'we can hardly find words to express' Christ's presence in the Eucharist, Trent taught:

> by the consecration of the bread and wine there takes place a change in the whole substance of bread into the substance of the body of Christ our Lord and of the whole substance of wine into the substance of his blood. This change the holy Catholic Church has fittingly and properly named transubstantiation.

This was an attempt to find some middle ground between a purely symbolic and an ultra-realist view of the presence of Christ's body and blood in the Eucharist.

In its Constitution on the Sacred Liturgy of 1963, the Second Vatican Council did not use the term 'transubstantiation' and listed various ways through which Christ is vitally present in liturgical celebrations. This presence comes to its highpoint with the consecrated bread and wine upon the altar and his encounter with Christians in sacramental communion.

The Eucharist as *sacrifice* became controversial much later than did the real presence of Christ in the Eucharist. St Cyprian of Carthage (d. 258) followed the Epistle to the Hebrews by calling Christ 'the high priest' who 'first offered himself as a sacrifice to the Father', and added that at the Eucharist 'the priest acts truly in Christ's stead...and offers a true and complete sacrifice to God the Father' (*Epistola* 63, 14).

St John Chrysostom (d. 407) insisted that there is only one sacrifice. Just as there are not 'many Christs' but only one in every place, so there is only 'one sacrifice': 'we offer now what was offered then, an inexhaustible offering...We offer the same sacrifice or rather we make a memorial of that sacrifice' (*In Hebreos*, 3. 17). The human ministers ('we who offer') are secondary, visible ministers of the invisible Christ: 'He who did this at the supper is the same who now performs the act. We rank as ministers; it is he who consecrates and transmutes the elements' (*In Mattheum*, 82). The belief that the Eucharist is the sacramental 're-presentation' of the one, historical sacrifice of Christ and, as a sacrifice, involves ordained priests remained more or less unchallenged until the 16th century.

Many Protestant Reformers denied the sacrificial nature of the Eucharist and spoke of a meal which recalled the loving self-sacrifice of Christ. They feared that admitting the sacrificial value of the Eucharist would belittle his unique sacrifice. By denying the sacrificial nature of the Eucharist, such Reformers logically regarded ordination to the priesthood as superfluous: no sacrifice, and so no priests. The Council of Trent dedicated its 22nd session (1562) to the sacrifice of the Mass. It restated traditional Catholic teaching: the bloody sacrifice Christ offered once and for all 'on the altar of the cross' is 'offered' in 'an unbloody manner', but not repeated, 'under visible signs' to celebrate 'the memory' of Christ's 'passage from this world' and to apply 'the salutary power' of his sacrifice 'for the forgiveness of sins' and 'other necessities' of the faithful.

In the 20th century, many Catholics and other Christians came to realize that it is a false choice to speak of the Eucharistic liturgy as either a sacrifice or a memorial meal. It is the sacrificial meal of the new covenant. A renewed sense of the reality conveyed by the term *anamnesis* (remembrance) helped. The Eucharist as *anamnesis* makes effective in the present the past event of Christ's sacrifice. It 're-presents' the whole event of his life, death, resurrection, and sending of the Holy Spirit, bringing that unique past to be powerfully present now.

The 20th century also brought further developments in appreciating the Eucharist: for instance, as empowering work for justice and peace. It retrieved, above all, a sense of the Eucharist as the 'fountain from which flows all the power of the Church' and 'the summit towards which her activity is directed' (Vatican II, *Sacrosanctum Concilium*, 10). Being the supreme way of glorifying God and bringing about the sanctification of human beings, the Eucharist proves the greatest of the sacraments and the central act of worship in the life of the Church.

Penance and the anointing of the sick

After presenting the three sacraments that together constitute Christian initiation, I take up two sacraments available for sinful and sick Catholics.

The forgiveness of sins was a key feature in the ministry of Jesus. He imparted the divine pardon not only through his words (e.g. Luke 7: 47–50), but also through his action of establishing table fellowship with sinners and reconciling them with God. After his resurrection from the dead and the outpouring of the Holy Spirit, people entered the Church through baptism. What, then, was the situation of baptized Christians who committed sins and even reverted to the sinful lifestyle they had renounced at their baptism? In passing, the Gospels indicate procedures to be followed for the 'brother who does wrong' (Matt. 18: 15–18). Paul shows his anxious concern over sins committed by Christians in Corinth and prescribes remedies. For example, a man who is living in concubinage with his stepmother should be expelled from the community, 'so that his spirit may be saved on the day of the Lord' (1 Cor. 5: 5). The apostle also writes of someone who has suffered for his wrongdoing, but now should be forgiven and reconciled with the community (2 Cor. 2: 5–8).

Early Christians distinguished between lesser and death-dealing sins. Daily sins could be forgiven through prayer (in particular, the Lord's Prayer), fasting, works of mercy, and the Eucharist. Such serious sins as apostasy and adultery, however, called for a public process of reconciliation that could happen only once in a lifetime. Such sinners publicly acknowledged their sins (confession), and were kept apart from community worship for a period of penance, contrite prayer, and almsgiving (satisfaction). The penitents asked for prayers from other members of the community. When the bishop judged the repentance adequate, he restored the sinners to full communion through the imposition of hands (absolution). Thus the administration of penance, as it emerged in the 3rd century, was a *public* action of reconciliation that led to a change of heart, involved the whole community, and was presided over by the bishop.

By the middle of the 5th century, however, this system had widely broken down—due to the vastly increased number of Christians, disruptions caused by the barbarian invasions, and other factors. The administration of penance was no longer totally public and limited to the ministry of bishops. Priests were delegated to be ministers of the sacrament, which now required strict secrecy.

The sacrament underwent an even more dramatic change from the end of the 6th century. Celtic and Anglo-Saxon monk-missionaries began fanning out across Europe, founding or re-founding Christian communities and introducing the 'monastic' practice of penance. This involved private confession to a spiritual father (or mother), an appropriate penance (which aimed more at restoring the balance of the moral universe than at reconciliation with the community), and a private prayer of pardon and blessing after the penance (or satisfaction for sins) was completed. Besides making the sacrament of penance a non-liturgical matter, the monk-missionaries put an end to the reconciliation for grave sins being available only once in a lifetime.

The severity of the penances imposed meant, however, that fewer Christians practised sacramental penance.

In an attempt to correct this situation, the Fourth Lateran Council (1215) prescribed that the faithful should '*at least* once a year confess all their sins in secret to their own priest' and receive communion (italics mine). The spread of the Dominican, Franciscan, and other orders in the 13th century made the practice of confession and communion more frequent. But many limited themselves to confession and communion once a year.

In 1439, the Council of Florence spelled out more fully what the sacrament of 'penance' involved:

(1) 'contrition of heart which requires that one be sorry for the sin committed with the resolve not to sin in the future';

(2) 'oral confession which requires that sinners confess to their priests in their integrity all the [serious] sins they remember';

(3) 'the words of absolution spoken by the priest who has authority to absolve'; and

(4) 'satisfaction for the sin according to the judgement of the priest, which is mainly achieved by prayer, fasting, and almsgiving'.

In 1551, in response to the claim of some Reformers that sinners needed only interior conversion, the Council of Trent emphasized the sacrament of penance and specified further details in the scheme of contrition, confession, absolution, and satisfaction. It encouraged a sense that the sacramental rite of penance was an affair between God and a sinful individual. What many Catholics largely ignored was the relevance to the community of what they came to call 'confession'. They considered the sacrament a private event and a means of personal grace. They failed to recognize that the sins of the baptized harm the Church. The once-in-a-lifetime penitential discipline of early Christianity was obviously severe, but it did appreciate both the damage baptized Christians do to the whole body of Christ by their sins and the fact that repentance means being reconciled with the worshipping community and sharing again fully in its life.

The Second Vatican Council signalled a recovery of a communal perspective: 'Those who approach the sacrament of penance receive pardon from the mercy of God . . . and at the same time are reconciled with the Church which they have wounded by their sins' (*Lumen Gentium*, 11). This renewed sense that sacramental penance reconciles sinners with God *and with the Church* shows up vividly in the three rites for celebrating the sacrament found in the 'Order of Penance' promulgated by Pope Paul VI in 1973. He significantly introduced a new name, 'the sacrament of reconciliation'. But this sacrament, which 're-presents' Christ's ministry to sinners, is still far from being fully used and appreciated by priests and people.

The anointing of the sick is a sacrament closely associated with that of reconciliation and also draws on the example of Christ. He showed his love for the sick and sinful by healing them and forgiving their sins (e.g. Mark 2: 1–12). The anointing of the sick took shape from the practice of Jesus and his first followers, and was inspired, in particular, by a passage from the Letter of James. The 'elders' had the specific role of 'praying over' the sick and anointing them with oil, understood to be endowed with special power from the Spirit. James invited the entire community to acknowledge their sinfulness and pray for one another. They should expect the power of the risen Lord to save, forgive, and heal the sick and sinful (Jas. 5: 14–16).

The sacrament came to be associated with the end of life and hence called 'extreme unction'. In 1439, the Council of Florence reflected this shift: 'this sacrament may not be given except to a sick person whose life is feared for'. The minister of the sacrament is a priest, and 'its effect is the healing of the mind and (as far as it is good for the soul) of the body as well'. In the 16th century, the Council of Trent followed the teaching of Florence when insisting on the sacramental status of 'extreme unction' against the Reformers. The sacrament is 'to be administered to the sick, especially to those who are so seriously ill that they seem near to death; hence it is also called the sacrament of the dying'.

When restoring the original name of the sacrament, 'the anointing of the sick', Vatican II emphasized that 'it is not a sacrament only for those who are at the point of death'. It can and should be received by those suffering from serious illness and the onset of old age (*Sacrosanctum Concilium*, 73). Through the 1972 rite for the anointing of the sick, this sacrament has come to be celebrated much more frequently, and with a number of people often receiving it together in church. While maintaining the promise of saving and healing expressed by the Letter of James, the new rite invites the sick and the old to associate their suffering with the redeeming mission of Jesus for the good of the Church and the whole world.

Sacraments in the service of communion

Authoritative ministry began with the mission of Jesus and the organization of early churches. The first Christians, while enjoying the basic equality of all the baptized, were, nevertheless, led and served by some who performed specific ministries for them.

The letters of St Ignatius of Antioch (d. around 107) clarify the nature of Christian life in Asia Minor: a united community gathered around one bishop, who was assisted by presbyters and deacons. A partly 3rd-century document, the *Apostolic Tradition* of Hippolytus, describes the ordination (conferred by the imposition of hands and the invocation of the Holy Spirit) and ministry of bishops, presbyters, and deacons. Its guidelines for these holy orders remain thoroughly recognizable today in the Catholic Church, among the Orthodox, and beyond.

In the late Middle Ages, serious questions arose about the sacramental power of bishops and priests and came to a head in the 16th century. Protestant Reformers, who insisted (rightly) that all the baptized share a *common* priesthood, denied a *special* sacrament of holy orders that derived from Christ and the New Testament Church. Ministry, many of them argued, was a function delegated by Christian communities to some of their members. In 1563, the Council of Trent, having upheld the sacrificial character of the Eucharist in its previous session (1562), insisted on the essential connection between sacrifice and priesthood: since 'the Catholic Church has received from the institution of Christ the holy, visible sacrifice of the Eucharist, it must also be acknowledged that there exists in the Church a new, visible, and external priesthood', which has 'the power of consecrating, offering, and administering his body and blood', as well as that of 'remitting sins'. The Council also maintained that bishops are 'superior' to priests, in as much as they 'govern the Church', 'ordain ministers', and 'confer the sacrament of confirmation'.

In a 1947 encyclical letter *Mediator Dei* ('the Mediator of God'), Pope Pius XII developed some teaching about holy orders that would prepare the way for the Second Vatican Council. All priesthood is founded in the one, unique priesthood of Christ, but the *ministerial* priesthood (conferred by the sacrament of holy orders) is to be distinguished from the *common* priesthood of all the faithful (conferred by baptism), and is exercised differently in the Eucharistic sacrifice, where priests 'act in the person of Christ'. At the same time, all share in the one sacrifice of Christ, with the people offering the sacrifice 'through' and 'with' the priests.

At Vatican II, a fresh attention to Christ's triple role as prophet/ herald, priest, and king/shepherd characterizes the Council's teaching on the common priesthood of the faithful, the ministry of bishops, and that of ordained priests. In particular, the prophetic, sanctifying, and pastoral role of presbyters means that their priesthood involves much more than merely fulfilling the cultic function exercised in offering the sacrifice of the Eucharist.

Finally, what of the sacrament of matrimony? How did Christian marriage find its place among the seven sacraments?

Jesus drew images from weddings for some of his parables (e.g. Matt. 21: 1–14; 25: 1–13). John's Gospel reports how Jesus attended a wedding (John 2: 1–11); the other Gospels show how Jesus safeguarded the institution of marriage by excluding divorce and remarriage as contrary to God's will (Mark 10: 2–12). The Letter to the Ephesians appealed to the union of all the baptized with Christ to encourage a startlingly elevated view of the loving relationship between husbands and wives. This powerful comparison implied the sacramental status of Christian marriage. Yet it took centuries for this implication to be fully elaborated.

From the 3rd century, Christians, while following the forms of marriage current in civil society, introduced some service of blessing and replaced the sacrificial rites of solemn Roman weddings with a celebration of the Eucharist. Moral teaching from the New Testament guided the way in which they lived out their married and family life. By the beginning of the second millennium, European rulers had turned over to bishops and their assistants the celebration of marriage and the administration of matrimonial matters. The liturgy for Christian marriage adopted many of the symbols used in civil ceremonies: for instance, the veil worn by the bride, her ring, and her joining hands with the bridegroom. The work of Thomas Aquinas and other medieval theologians clarified finally the sacramental status of Christian marriage. Hence in 1274 the Second Council of Lyons listed marriage among the seven sacraments.

Many Protestant Reformers, while maintaining the holiness of marriage, denied its sacramental status and rejected the juridical function of the Church in matrimonial matters. The Council of Trent in 1563 upheld the marriage of Christians as a sacrament instituted by Christ, whose 'grace perfects the natural love' of a married couple, 'confirms' their 'indissoluble union, and sanctifies' them. It insisted on the competence of the official Church in such matrimonial matters as the right to determine necessary conditions for contracting a valid marriage. The priest who blessed the marriage was understood to be an official witness and not the minister of the sacrament. Hence marriage stands apart from the other sacraments, in as much as those who 'minister' to each other are the bride and bridegroom (Figure 5).

The Second Vatican Council put married life within the context of all the baptized being called to holiness—married people, no less than celibate priests and consecrated religious men and women (*Lumen Gentium*, 39–42). Vatican II went beyond Trent by calling marriage an 'intimate partnership of life and love' that involves 'total fidelity' and 'unbreakable unity' and by highlighting the importance of sexual love for the complete marriage relationship (*Gaudium et Spes*, 48–9).

The Catholic Church and her mission

The first part of this chapter has described the sacramental life of the Church. But official teaching about the nature and mission of the Church flowered late—only in the 19th and 20th centuries.

The heart of Jesus' preaching was the Kingdom of God, which will be forever a more encompassing reality than the Church. Nevertheless, from the 2nd century it was the institutional Church that needed to be defended. Irenaeus called it 'the seven-branch candlestick which bears the light of Christ' (*Adversus Haereses*, 5. 20. 1). He thus referred to the origin of the Church in the Jewish people and implied the role of Jesus in founding this new assembly

5. A Catholic wedding in Nairobi, Kenya.

of God's people. Without proposing any detailed blueprint for the life and structures of the Church, Jesus intended to build another Temple 'not made with hands' (Mark 14: 58; 15: 29), to introduce a universal covenant through his death and resurrection, and, by his choice of the Twelve headed by Peter, to reform the twelve tribes of Israel, and through them bring divine salvation to all the nations. Jesus was the Founder (upper case) of the Church, whereas the Twelve, Paul, and other apostles were the founders (lower case). All Christians of the 1st century can be considered to have been in a variety of ways the founding fathers and founding mothers of the Church.

Irenaeus saw the Church as *one* by following 'one and the same way of salvation'; *holy* through 'the Spirit of God'; *catholic* in preaching 'the truth everywhere' and encompassing 'the whole world'; and *apostolic* by enjoying the 'true and solid' tradition coming through the bishops from the apostles (*Adversus Haereses*, 3. 24; 5. 20). The 4th-century Nicene-Constantinopolitan Creed enshrined unity, holiness, catholicity, and apostolicity as the four 'marks', or essential characteristics, of the Church. But we find them already endorsed 200 years earlier by Irenaeus. He insisted perhaps most of all on 'apostolicity', stressing a lasting fidelity to the foundations of Christian faith taught by Peter, Paul, and the other apostles.

From the early 5th century, barbarian invasions ravaged Europe and parts of North Africa. From the early 7th century, Muslim forces began to take over much of the Middle East; by the early 8th century, Islam had taken possession of North Africa and Spain. In those turbulent times, the spiritual and, to some extent, the political authority of the bishop of Rome developed. The primacy of Peter and his successors was supported by appeals to the language of Matthew 16: 18–19 about the founding of the Church on the rock of Peter and his being given the keys of the Kingdom. At the Council of Chalcedon in 451, after the bishops had listened to the Letter to Flavian written by Pope Leo I, they exclaimed: 'Peter has spoken through the mouth of Leo.'

From the 6th century, the title of 'patriarch' was given to the bishops of Rome, Constantinople, Alexandria, Antioch, and Jerusalem. The patriarchs exercised wide authority in such matters as appointing bishops of major dioceses and judging appeals to their jurisdiction. For Leo the Great, Gregory the Great (pope 590–604), and other leading popes in the first millennium, the bishop of Rome was the centre of unity in the true faith and the last court of appeal in matters involving this faith. Various forces conspired to bring a tragic break, traditionally dated to the mutual excommunications of July 1054, between the patriarch of Constantinople, or Ecumenical Patriarch, and the bishop of Rome, or Patriarch of the West.

The centralizing policies of Gregory VII (pope 1073–85) and Innocent III (pope 1198–1216) involved claims to exercise jurisdiction over the whole Church and even to dictate to temporal rulers in major secular matters. The armies of popes were involved in wars—right down to the unification of Italy in 1870. Thanks to John XXIII, John Paul II, and other modern popes, the complete military irrelevance of the papacy has coincided with its greatest moral authority. In a world that continues to be ravaged by war, the loss of the papal states in 1870 has led to the pope becoming the incumbent of the world's most prominent and influential religious office. Over 170 nations have entered diplomatic relations with the tiny Vatican State; presidents, prime ministers, and other political leaders arrive regularly for meetings with the pope, who constantly urges the cause of peace.

All of this has happened despite Christendom being divided, first by the 11th-century break with the Orthodox, and then in the 16th century. The Protestant Reformers, headed by Martin Luther, rejected papal authority in their campaign to bring the Church into line with New Testament faith, but did not (at least initially) envisage a divided Christendom. Although it was called to clarify teaching and reform abuses, the Council of Trent dealt with other issues and not directly with questions of the Church and the papacy.

In a world shaken by the French Revolution and social unrest, many rulers continued to promote the independence of national churches at the expense of wider Christian unity. Catholics looked for a stronger papacy to check abuses and save Christianity from lapsing into religious indifference. At the First Vatican Council (1869–70), the bishops solemnly approved two pieces of teaching about the papal office: first, a primacy of jurisdiction over the whole Church; and secondly, papal infallibility.

Primacy was understood to confer a universal authority that allowed the pope to intervene anywhere, without depending on the permission of the local bishop. The Council added, however, that this papal primacy was intended to support and not belittle the God-given authority of bishops in their dioceses.

Infallibility concerned a possibility for the teaching office of the pope that has rarely been exercised: for instance, in the 1950 solemn definition by Pius XII of the assumption of the Blessed Virgin Mary—namely, that at the end of her earthly life she was taken up, body and soul, into heavenly glory. An infallible teaching is one that invokes the fullness of papal authority (*ex cathedra*) as universal pastor and successor of St Peter, and concerns some revealed truth that all Christians should believe. Hence such papal infallibility is not involved when the pope teaches on matters other than revealed faith and morals. Nor can infallibility be recognized when it is not manifestly clear that the pope wants to teach *ex cathedra*. Thus the 1968 encyclical on married life and love, *Humanae Vitae* ('Of human life'), which rejected the use of artificial means of birth control, cannot be considered an exercise of the infallible teaching office. Paul VI never claimed that, nor did he use the language which would warrant it being considered *ex cathedra* teaching.

By concentrating on papal primacy and infallibility, Vatican I left much to be completed. In its Constitution on the Church (*Lumen Gentium*) and other documents, Vatican II filled out some teaching on the nature and function of the Church in herself and in her relations with others. At least five points should be retrieved.

(1) For many centuries, a sharp distinction prevailed between clergy and laity, as if there were two classes of Christians. Even today, many people ignore the fact that all the baptized make up the Church, and speak of 'the Church' when they mean only the bishops and priests. Vatican II insisted that *all* the baptized constitute the People of God and are equally called to holiness and to participate in the mission of the Church.

(2) The images of the Body of Christ, People of God, and Temple of the Holy Spirit witness to the rich reality of the Church. No single description can by itself express adequately all that the Church is and should be.

(3) The reign of God, despite recurrent challenges and setbacks, is steadily growing to its final completion. The Church exists for this Kingdom, and is to be understood in its light, and not vice versa.

(4) The Church is simultaneously holy and sinful, and must constantly 'follow the path of penitence and renewal' (*Lumen Gentium*, 8).

(5) A teaching role and responsibility for the whole Church belongs to the entire college of bishops through their episcopal ordination and being in communion with the bishop of Rome. While this 'collegiality' is a new term, it comes from the original college of apostles led by St Peter.

Finally, Vatican II launched a new era in the Catholic Church's relations with other Christian communities, with Jews, and with the followers of world religions. Dialogue with these 'others' has already produced much fruit. But the healing of so many divisions in the Christian and human family remains a matter of prayerful hope and generous commitment.

Chapter 5
Catholic moral life and teaching

How should Catholics behave? What principles should guide their moral life? How might the holiness with which they have been blessed express itself in their daily existence?

At its best, Catholic teaching on the moral life is noble and convincing, as in a summary statement from John Paul II's 1993 encyclical *Veritatis Splendor* ('The splendour of truth'): 'Jesus' way of acting and his words—his deeds and his precepts—constitute the moral rule of Christian life.' At its worst, some teachers have deformed that teaching. The liberal views of Antonino Diana (1586–1663), for instance, could accommodate various forms of human violence and robbery. That led to his being nicknamed 'the lamb of God', since in his own way he could 'take away the sins of the world'. He has his latter-day successors: for example, in such Catholic thinkers who 'generously' extend just-war theory even to recommend pre-emptive strikes.

Historical developments

Jesus and the authors of the New Testament maintained much moral teaching that they had inherited from the Old Testament. Jesus innovated by putting together in one love-command the hitherto distinct commandments to love God (Deut. 6: 5) and to love one's neighbour (Lev. 19: 18), by teaching a love for one's enemies (Matt. 5: 43–8), and by practising an equality that was shockingly new in that women belonged to the travelling band of his disciples (Luke 8: 1–3). But, in general, Jesus, Paul, and other early Christians endorsed what Judaism had taught about right and wrong behaviour, above all through the Ten Commandments. Jesus and his first followers, however, never endorsed armed violence, as did some texts in the Hebrew Bible.

The *Didache* shows that a lengthy catechesis on moral matters had emerged by the end of the 1st century. Both the *Didache* and the roughly contemporary *Epistle of Barnabas* contrasted 'the way of life' with 'the way of death'. Their respect for life included rejecting abortion and infanticide, both of which were widely practised by non-Christians.

A straight line leads from this very early teaching to the Second Vatican Council, which described abortion and infanticide as 'abominable crimes' (*Gaudium et Spes*, 51), and to John Paul II's *Evangelium Vitae* ('The gospel of life'). His concern for life rejected abortion as 'a grave moral disorder' and a decision 'against the weakest and most defenceless of human beings' (nos. 28, 62, 70). He repudiated a 'culture of death', which countenances euthanasia (in such forms as physician-assisted suicide) and killing or deliberately shortening the life of handicapped infants.

Evangelium Vitae also pleaded for life in two further ways. It called 'the use of human embryos or foetuses' for experiments 'a crime against their dignity as human beings who have a right to the same respect owed to a child once born' (no. 63). It excluded the death penalty, 'except in the case of absolute necessity', or 'when it would not be possible otherwise to defend society'. The pope added: 'today, however, as a result of steady improvements in the organization of the penal system, such cases are very rare, if not practically non-existent' (no. 56).

In the centuries that followed the *Didache*, Christian leaders continued to address moral issues. Augustine of Hippo (d. 430), for instance, gave the highest importance to truth-telling and condemned lying as something that could not be justified by allegedly good intentions. He needs to be heard in a world where truth, at best, has often become a fairly trifling affair and, at worst, is systematically distorted and perverted. Some teachers, like Pope Gregory the Great (d. 604), spelled out the seven deadly sins, or sins traditionally considered to be the root of all other sins: pride, avarice or covetousness, lust, envy, gluttony, anger, and sloth. In the Middle Ages, Thomas Aquinas (d. 1274) followed Aristotle in discussing the virtues needed for human flourishing—a theme that has been retrieved in modern ethics. He also encouraged thinking about the 'natural law', constituted by those universally valid moral principles which are discoverable by human reason and should govern social institutions and personal morality. Dante (d. 1321) brought together doctrine and a detailed account of the moral life. In his *Divine Comedy,* he constructed the long climb up the mountain of purgatory around seven terraces on which sinners are cleansed of the seven deadly sins.

It was not, however, until modern times that theologians and official teachers began developing a distinct body of moral teaching. For centuries they endorsed a broadly agreed version of the virtuous life. This largely unchallenged moral consensus tolerated, however, the use of torture and the institution of slavery. In the case of criminals and suspected heretics, popes and theologians, almost without exception, accepted the use of torture. A firm rejection of any 'physical and mental torture' finally came in the Second Vatican Council's teaching on respect for the human person (*Gaudium et Spes*, 27). Notoriously, many governments, so long as they can escape adverse criticism, still practise or allow torture to be practised by their security forces and, if necessary, 'outsource' such 'advanced interrogation techniques' to less publicly accountable countries.

Their Jewish heritage and the widespread presence of slaves in Graeco-Roman society did nothing to encourage the first Christians to question the institution of slavery, even if they moderated its worst features. Some New Testament letters contained rules of conduct for Christian slave-owners as well as slaves: 'Masters, treat your slaves justly and fairly, for you know that you also have a Master in heaven' (Col. 4: 1). Across Christian Europe, slavery was gradually transformed into the much milder system of serfdom. Sadly, the discovery of America by Columbus in 1492 initiated a new period of slave-traffic and slave-owning. Pope Paul III in 1537 and other popes condemned the slave trade. But many Catholics continued to consider slavery compatible with the natural law and justifiable under certain circumstances. In the name of the essential equality of all human beings, Vatican II denounced 'any kind of slavery, whether social or political' (*Gaudium et Spes*, 29). In his encyclical *Veritatis Splendor*, John Paul II called slavery 'intrinsically evil' (no. 80). In retrospect, one can see how Catholics continued to draw their moral standards about slavery at least in part from existing social patterns. They failed for centuries to see what was demanded by Christ's love-command and by their belief that all human beings have been created in the divine image and likeness.

One can add further examples of developments in Catholic moral doctrine: first, the teaching on social justice developed by Pope Leo XIII and his successors; secondly, the teaching on universal human rights (and their correlative duties) set out in John XXIII's 1963 encyclical *Pacem in Terris* ('Peace on earth') and vigorously elaborated by John Paul II; and thirdly, the sensitivity (which emerged after Vatican II) to ecological issues and the retrieval from Francis of Assisi (d. 1226) of a love for nature that excludes the dangerous abuse of the earth and its resources. Our planet cannot continue to be a life-giving environment unless human beings quickly become much more responsible stewards of the created world. The 2015 encyclical letter on ecology and climate issued by Pope Francis, *Laudato Si'* ('Praise be [to you, my Lord!]'), highlighted the urgency of caring for our common home.

Such developments of Catholic moral teaching have come slowly, sometimes with shameful slowness. Yet they illustrate a willingness to learn what the divine love revealed in Jesus Christ demands of his followers. The results of those developments reached a provisional highpoint with Vatican II's 1965 Pastoral Constitution on the Church in the Modern World. This was the first fairly complete Catholic document on the moral life to come from a council or a pope.

We can track several moral convictions rooted in Catholic thinking and behaviour. I am not alleging that these convictions are unique to Catholicism, but only that they are distinctive and persistent.

Respect for life

Vatican II and John Paul II showed a deep concern to elaborate a consistent ethic in support of human dignity and life. The Constitution on the Church in the Modern World devoted a whole chapter to the fostering of peace and establishing an effective community of nations (nos. 77–90). The Council, in the face of new weapons that 'can inflict immense and indiscriminate havoc', called for 'a completely fresh appraisal of war', and endorsed condemnations of 'total war' (which had already come from Pius XII, John XXIII, and Paul VI). The Council also condemned as 'frightful crimes' the 'extermination' of entire races, nations, or ethnic minorities (*Gaudium et Spes*, 79–80). It had in mind here the six million Jewish victims of Nazi genocide, an unspeakable crime that John Paul II made a repeated theme of speeches and sermons.

Gaudium et Spes, along with a concern to 'curb the savagery of war', nevertheless acknowledged that 'as long as the danger of war persists and there is no international authority with the necessary competence and power, governments cannot be denied the right of lawful self-defence, *once all peace efforts have failed* (*Gaudium et Spes*, 79; italics mine). This was tantamount to accepting the possibility of a just defence (to be distinguished from holy wars, crusades, and pre-emptive strikes). But in some tragic recent examples, war has been declared not only before exhausting all efforts at peace but also in the cause of national self-aggrandizement.

Respect for human life characterizes the best features of the Catholic tradition—right from the early teaching in support of 'the way of life' provided by the *Didache* and the *Epistle of Barnabas* down to Pope Francis—that shows respect for life to be a distinctive (but not unique) characteristic of Catholic morality.

The sexual order

Men and women were both created in the image and likeness of God and can find through marriage their human and religious fulfilment. From the start of Christianity, respect for the personal and social values of human sexuality and a desire to nourish healthy family life underpinned a teaching that defended a middle ground between two extremes: a widespread licentiousness and shameful treatment of women, on the one hand, and the belittling of the goodness of married people's sexual life that came from such groups as the Manicheans and the Cathars, on the other.

In the immediate post-New Testament period, we find the *Didache* and the *Epistle of Barnabas* warning against 'the way of darkness' by repudiating three kinds of sexual activity that the Catholic tradition would consistently repudiate—premarital sex, extramarital sex, and homosexual practices: 'You shall not commit fornication; you shall not commit adultery; you shall not engage in homosexual activity' (*Epistle of Barnabas*, 19. 4; *Didache*, 2. 2). In all three cases, down through the ages many Catholics have dissented from this teaching. But in doing so, they have been overriding the judgement of the New Testament scriptures and the mainstream tradition. But what of sexuality and Catholic married life?

From the time of Pius XI's encyclical letter *Casti Connubii* ('Of chaste marriage'), Catholic teaching has tried to hold together the two purposes of marital intercourse: the fostering of mutual love and the begetting of children. Clearly tensions will arise between these two purposes. Responsible parenthood must reckon with such factors as the lack of proper housing for a larger family, the precarious health of one or other of the spouses, economic difficulties, and the dramatic growth in the world's population. Pius XI recognized the legitimacy of natural family planning (or choosing the safe or sterile period for intercourse), but rejected medical contraception.

Vatican II couched its teaching in general terms, encouraging in spouses 'a sense of human and Christian responsibility'. With 'docile reverence towards God' and 'common counsel and effort', they should reach 'a right judgement' about having further children (*Gaudium et Spes*, 50-1). Methods of birth control were discussed not by the Council but by a commission of experts. In 1966, they presented a final report to Pope Paul VI; a strong majority on the commission recommended a change in the teaching coming from Pius XI. Paul VI did not, however, follow this advice. In his 1968 encyclical *Humanae Vitae* ('Of human life'), while recognizing the importance of married love and endorsing responsible parenthood, he rejected contraception. He appealed to the inseparable connection between the unitive and procreative meaning of sexual intercourse, and declared that 'each and every marriage act' must be open to the transmission of life (no. 11). While being an authoritative statement, the encyclical was not an infallible document. The bishops of many countries, including Cardinal Albino Luciani of Venice (to become Pope John Paul I in 1978), introduced mitigating nuances into the papal teaching and would not unconditionally exclude artificial means of birth control.

John Paul II, while saying nothing about any means adopted, repeatedly condemned contraception as gravely wrong. He also firmly distinguished contraception from abortion as *'specifically different* evils'. Unlike contraception, abortion 'directly violates the divine commandment: "You shall not kill"' (*Evangelium Vitae*, 13; italics his).

Around the world, innumerable Catholic couples, after prayer and reflection, have conscientiously decided what responsible parenthood requires of them. Here they can be encouraged by the words of Vatican II: 'it is the spouses themselves who must ultimately make this judgement' (*Gaudium et Spes*, 50). They can be encouraged also by the fact that neither the Bishops' Synod on marriage and family life in its *Final Report* (October 2015) nor Pope Francis in *Amoris Laetitia* (March 2016) repeated the teaching of Paul VI in *Humanae Vitae* (1968) and John Paul II in *Familiaris Consortio* (1981) that 'each and every marriage act must remain open to the transmission of life'. These two popes had argued, albeit in different ways, that contraception is 'unnatural' and compromises marital love.

Many Catholics, however, wonder about deeming responsible contraception necessarily unloving and 'unnatural', irrespective of the circumstances and intentions of the couple. Procedures of modern medicine that involve drastic surgery, the insertion of tubes into the body, chemotherapy, and the rest can look 'unnatural'. But it is precisely their 'God-given' and educated nature that leads doctors to use such procedures.

Those who judge what is 'natural' and 'unnatural' sometimes put together (heterosexual) contraceptive practices and (homosexual) same-sex acts as both being genital acts against our God-given nature. But I have not found a serious study of criteria that would convincingly distinguish between what is 'natural' (and so morally acceptable) and 'unnatural' (or morally unacceptable). Apropos of homosexual couples, unlike heterosexual couples, they cannot, left to themselves or 'naturally', produce babies. Since Catholics believe that the purpose of marriage is not only loving companionship but also procreation, what is to be said about same-sex marriage, which the Catholic Church does not accept but which became legal in England and Wales from March 2014 and in the Republic of Ireland from November 2015—not to mention other countries?

In non-confessional democracies those who do not accept same-sex marriage need to distinguish between their personal faith convictions and what the state, backed by the majority of its citizens, might decide. Are same-sex couples sufficiently protected legally by their entering civil partnerships? During the first two years after same-sex marriages became legal in England and Wales, 15,000 same-sex couples went through a marriage ceremony. Of these just over half (7,732) converted from civil partnership to marriage. Obviously they desired a marriage ceremony above a civil partnership. Like many other gay and lesbian couples, they felt discriminated against by being refused marriage equality. However, since same-sex marriage has only recently become an option, it is not currently known how same-sex marriages will compare as permanent and exclusive unions with heterosexual marriages.

Redefining marriage to include same-sex marriage carries implications for society at large. Questions that have been asked include whether all registered marriage celebrants should be obliged to officiate at homosexual marriages, even if it contradicts their religious beliefs. There is also controversy surrounding the issue of adoption. If gay and lesbian couples approach adoption agencies, should those agencies, irrespective of their beliefs, be compelled by law to provide children? For those who believe that same-sex parents should not be allowed to adopt, questions are again raised, for instance, when an existing close relationship to an orphaned child would mean that adoption by a particular same-sex couple could actually be the best solution for *this* child.

Some of the issues which arise concerning the disclosure of biological parentage to children conceived by a heterosexual couple through IVF (involving a donor of sperm or an ovum) may also attend same-sex parents. As in IVF for some heterosexual couples, a lesbian couple needs only a sperm donor to 'start a family'. Will the children of donated sperms have the right to know their biological father? Gay couples have to secure an ovum and a surrogate mother. Will the children of these procedures have the right to know the woman who supplied the ovum and the mother who carried them for nine months in her womb? What rights belong to these two women, or one woman in the case of the surrogate mother also supplying the ovum?

A further question has been raised by some Catholics: do children have the right to be brought up by a mother and a father? Research has not yet established the outcomes for children of same-sex marriages. But the questions trouble many believers. Can the quality of love shown them by two mothers or two fathers ensure children's happy growth to human maturity? Or, in general, do children do better when reared by their biological mother and father?

Justice and charity

The Christian tradition has called justice a *cardinal* ('hinge') virtue, because right human conduct pivots upon it. Thomas Aquinas described justice as 'the strong and firm will to give each his due'. From the time of Leo XIII's encyclical *Rerum Novarum* of 1891 and its insistence on what justice demands for 'the interests of the poorer populations', social justice became a key theme in Catholic teaching. It aims to remove whatever excludes groups and individuals from participating in society and leaves them living on the margins of society. Love, even more than considerations of justice, has inspired Christians to care for any man or woman in need. Christianity inherited from the Old Testament a healthy concern for widows, orphans, and strangers, along with prophetic opposition to those who oppressed the economically and socially weak. Jesus expected his followers to help the hungry, the thirsty, strangers, the naked, the sick, and prisoners (Matt. 25: 31–46). His parable of the Good Samaritan called for a willingness to reach across religious and cultural divides to assist any human being in distress (Luke 10: 30–7).

The words of Jesus have stimulated innumerable Catholics to open hospitals—not least, women who belong to religious institutes founded to care for the sick, the aged, and the terminally ill. A parallel commitment to the work of educating children, young people, and adults has been fired by the sense of Jesus' saying: 'I was ignorant and you taught me.'

Forming our conscience

John Paul II called conscience 'the proximate norm of personal morality' (*Veritatis Splendor*, 60). This statement cohered with a long Catholic tradition and with the teaching of Vatican II: 'In the depths of their conscience human beings detect a law which they do not make for themselves but which they must obey. Its voice always summons them to love and to do what is good and to shun what is evil.' The Council also realistically recognized the attitude of all those who 'take little care to seek what is true and good' and whose conscience 'through a habit of sin' gradually becomes 'almost blind' (*Gaudium et Spes*, 16). Paul states the remedy. Our sinful minds need to be renewed by the Holy Spirit before we can 'discern the will of God' and know 'what is good, acceptable, and perfect' (Rom. 12: 2).

The moral law needs to be applied to the concrete circumstances of life if we are to decide conscientiously on what is to be done

(*Veritatis Splendor*, 54–64). This is far from endorsing a facile self-determination that claims the right to determine for oneself 'the criteria of good and evil and then acts accordingly' (*Veritatis Splendor*, 32). Forming one's conscience means attending with utter seriousness to the divine law and letting it shape one's life. Jesus wanted nothing less from his followers (Mark 7: 20–3).

Following one's conscience converges with following Christ and taking to heart his generously self-forgetful style of life. St Paul pointed to Christ as the supreme moral exemplar. St Irenaeus expressed beautifully what such discipleship entails:

> There is no other way for us to learn than to see our Teacher and hear his voice with our own ears. It is by becoming imitators of his actions and doers of his words—that we may have communion with him. (*Adversus Haereses*, 5. 1. 1)

Chapter 6
Characteristics of Catholicism

Catholicism varies considerably around the world. To sense the diversity it would be enough to start from Catania (Sicily) and its exuberant observance of the feast of St Agatha (5 February), visit Kerala (South India) and attend Mass in a Syro-Malabar church, and travel further to the highlands of Papua New Guinea and share in a Sunday Eucharist celebrated in pidgin. The culturally, geographically, and ritually diverse character of Catholic worship and life raises the question: What holds it all together? Which authentically Catholic instincts and concerns shape and unify the world's oldest and largest institution that has spread almost everywhere? Is there such a thing as an identifiable Catholic worldview, and are there characteristics of Catholicism that show through the variety of cultural and ritual expressions of Catholic life around the globe?

One might point to governance by bishops (assisted by priests and deacons) who, by leading their dioceses and remaining in communion with the bishop of Rome, keep the Catholic Church together. Or one could name the celebration of the seven sacraments and, above all, the Eucharist ('the sacrament of sacraments', Thomas Aquinas) as the force that identifies and unites Catholics everywhere. There is a special Catholic emphasis on attending the Sunday Eucharist, and there is a particular Catholic intensity about receiving Christ in Holy Communion and praying before his presence in the Blessed Sacrament. Among Catholics everywhere, the Eucharist focuses commitment to Christ and acts as a powerful collective force. Many teachers used to quote the summary of Irish faith and practice offered by Augustine Birrell (Chief Secretary for Ireland from 1908 to 1916) in a report that he sent to London: 'it is the Mass that matters'.

But can we dive deeper and name characteristics that pervade Catholic worship, belief, and practice? We can name three such characteristics: a desire to incorporate all material reality into their sacramental and devotional life, a willingness to practise the principle of 'both/and', and a deep concern for unity.

The material world and God's grace

At the birth of Christianity, St Paul's Letter to the Romans bears witness to the transforming light of the good news and the power of baptism (and the other sacraments) brought to bear on a sinful world. Before the reading or singing of the Gospel, Catholics make the sign of the cross on their foreheads, mouth, and breast. That is a vivid way of declaring that the message of the crucified Christ should heal and transform their thoughts, words, and affections. At the same time, the sacraments themselves witness to the God-oriented character of all created reality, an orientation that has been radically enhanced by the incarnation. The material world has become even more the theatre of divine grace and mediates God's blessings.

Catholic Christianity has fostered the sense that all human reality and, indeed, the whole material cosmos have been blessed and changed by the 'Word becoming flesh' (John 1: 14). From the 2nd century AD, Gnostics have taken redemption to mean the human spirit escaping from the body and from an evil, material world. Against such aberrations, St Irenaeus refused to downplay matter. He insisted on the goodness of the created world in general and of the human body in particular. An essential dignity has been conferred on our bodies not only through their origin (in God's creation) and their destiny (in the resurrection to come) but also (and even more) through the incarnation of the Son of God. By assuming 'flesh' (the complete human condition of body and spirit), the Son of God ratified the inherent value of men and women created in God's image and likeness (Gen. 1: 26–7).

Material realities, such as water, bread, wine, oil, and human bodies, have now been lifted to a new level and spiritualized, so as to become the channels of God's self-revelation and bearers of the divine holiness. Through the seven sacraments of the Church, things that we can see, hear, touch, taste, and smell impart the divine truth and power. The water poured in baptism, bread and wine consecrated at the Eucharist, hands imposed in ordination, oil smeared on the foreheads and hands of the sick, bodies joined in matrimony, and other perceptible signs that constitute the sacraments communicate spiritual blessings and a share in the life of the tripersonal God. The sacraments of the Catholic Church transfigure the material elements and actions of a world that is already 'charged with the grandeur of God' (Gerard Manley Hopkins, 'God's Grandeur').

The sacramentalizing of the material world and of human life finds its heart in the seven sacraments that initiate and nourish a share in the life of the all-holy God. But this spiritualizing of the world and human beings extends beyond the seven sacraments: in particular, to such sacramentals (material things that become sacred signs) as the ashes Catholics receive on their foreheads on Ash Wednesday and the palms they carry home on Palm Sunday. In the proper sense, sacramentals are holy practices, prayers, and all manner of popular devotions and objects officially approved and blessed in the Catholic Church. They include some of the traditions that were fostered by Franciscans and Dominicans and have never lost their popularity: for example, making the Stations of the Cross (especially during the weeks leading up to Good

Friday), Christmas cribs, which recall Christ's birth among us, and the saying of the rosary.

Structures (catacombs, churches, and monasteries) and religious art played their part in sacralizing life right from the early centuries of Catholic Christianity. Obviously, buildings and visual images have remained central to the performance of official worship. But even when the sacraments are not being administered, churches, paintings, statues, mosaics, altarpieces, and stained-glass windows are there to lift to God the minds and hearts of those who visit. For Eastern Christians, both Orthodox and Catholics, icons are endued with divine power and help the whole world to symbolize God.

Some of the very old sacramentals, such as the palms distributed on Palm Sunday, derive from the history of Jesus—in this case, from his entrance into Jerusalem shortly before he died (Mark 11: 8). Other sacramentals, such as the usage of sweet-smelling incense, go back even further, in this case to rites practised in the Jerusalem Temple (Ps. 141: 2). The scented smoke of burning incense that rose to God meant 'squandering' something costly in a gift of unreserved love. Incense has maintained a central place in the worship of Orthodox Christians. Catholics use it frequently: in processions, at the celebration of Mass, and for funeral rites.

Saints and their earthly stories also play a part in spiritualizing the year and the movement of human life, as well as in supporting a sense of national identity. It can be a matter of celebrating annually the feast day of a saint who has a special connection with some nation, city, village, parish, shrine, or person. On 17 March, Irish Catholics around the world continue to celebrate the feast of St Patrick; Scots and those of Scottish origin do the same on 30 November, the feast of St Andrew, their patron saint. On 13 June, Italians pack into Padua for the feast of St Antony (d. 1231), a Franciscan friar who spent the last years of his life in or near that city. Many Catholics, year by year, observe their 'name day', the feast day of the saint after whom they are called. Although the day of their birth may not coincide with the feast day of their saint, it is the feast day that often counts for more with them and their families. Sometimes the special 'function' of a saint figures prominently on the feast day. Thus St Antony (d. 356), an Egyptian Christian who organized the life of hermits in the desert, is celebrated in Italy and elsewhere as a protector of animals—and, by extension, of goldfish, canaries, and other pets. On his feast day, 17 January, the Mass ends with wine and sweet bread being distributed to the faithful as they leave the church, while an assortment of animals receives a blessing outside (and sometimes inside).

Around the world, Catholics use a wide variety of blessings for their homes, their workplaces, and other material things that enter their lives and should be consecrated to become part of joining Christ in a pilgrimage home to God. Thus there are blessings for factories, farms, homes, hospitals, libraries, offices, shops, aircraft, motor cars, and ships (including fishing fleets). Blessings are available for engaged couples, families, nurses and doctors (with their patients), teachers (along with students at the beginning of the academic year), travellers, and further categories of persons. The urbanizing of the world and the flight from the land may have meant, for a while, a decline in such practices. But now blessings seem to be booming again, and many families treasure, for example, the annual blessing of their homes at Easter-tide. Through such sacramentals, the powerful presence of Christ in every aspect of bodily and human existence can become more perceptible for families.

Daily life can be spiritualized and 'sacramentalized' through the statues of Jesus or his saints in their sitting-room or kitchen and images on the walls of their bedrooms and elsewhere in their homes. For Christians everywhere, the family forms the utterly essential group within society. The future of the world and the

Church depends on this sacred unit. Many Catholic (and other Christian) families draw inspiration from Christmas cribs in their homes; at the heart of these cribs are three figures: the newborn Jesus, Mary, and Joseph, her husband and the legal father of Jesus.

The sanctification of *time* goes together with the seven sacraments and the innumerable sacramentals that turn material signs into means for mediating the divine gifts. Such sanctification happens, of course, through the Eucharistic celebration of the feasts and seasons of the liturgical year (above all, Advent, Christmas, Lent, and Easter). But time is also sanctified through the Liturgy of the Hours, when Catholics and other Christians gather at different hours of day or night in cathedrals, parish churches, monasteries, and other places to hear passages of scripture (and other sacred writings) being read and to sing or recite together psalms and further prayers. Those who follow the daily programme of official worship give praise to God, share in Christ's priestly office, and intercede for the salvation of the whole world. Vatican II's first document, *Sacrosanctum Concilium*, sets out beautifully how the divine office or Liturgy of the Hours sanctifies the passing of time on a daily and annual basis.

This section has laid the ground for what follows. It is typically Catholic to embrace 'both/and', and hold together things that some other Christians may tend to oppose to each other. Hence Catholics, like Orthodox Christians, do not accept an 'either/or' in the case of the sacraments and sacramental practices that we have just summarized above.

Sacramentals remain subordinate to baptism, the Eucharist, and the other five sacraments, but belong with them in consecrating to God through Christ the whole of bodily and human existence. There are numerous examples of the characteristically Catholic readiness to hold together what others separate or even oppose.

Jesus and Mary

Like members of Orthodox Churches, Catholics do not accept an 'either/or' in the case of Jesus and his Mother. Many Protestant Reformers and their followers hold that honouring Mary (and, for that matter, other saints) somehow blurs the unique role of Jesus as Saviour. But Catholics do not admit a choice here; they want Jesus *and* his Mother. This instinct has prompted them into erecting in different parts of the world wayside scenes of Calvary. At the foot of the cross, Christ's Mother keeps her lonely vigil.

Catholics, Orthodox, and some other Christians feel themselves understood and cherished by this woman and mother. A 4th-century Greek papyrus gives us in a Greek version the first text of *Sub Tuum Presidium*, one of the oldest Christian prayers after those found in the Bible. It begins: 'Beneath your protective shelter we flee, holy Mother of God.' This prayer, in an expanded form, has continued to be used right down to the present day. Like the rosary with its joyful, sorrowful, and glorious mysteries—and, since 2002, mysteries of light—that commemorate the main stages in the story of Christ, the *Sub Tuum Presidium* moves from Mary to her Son. Like this prayer, exquisite Marian antiphons (e.g. the *Salve Regina*), classical compositions for the *Magnificat* and *Ave Maria*, statues of Mary with her Son (Figure 6), stained-glass portrayals from medieval Europe, and Eastern icons from all centuries present Marian devotion at its best and truest. Mary's beauty, nobility, and importance are all derived through the Holy Spirit from her Son.

Both a 'vertical' and a 'horizontal' love

A Catholic 'both/and', shared by other Christians, concerns the love of God and love of one's neighbour. Catholics want to give time to God in prayer, either alone or with others, but they also want to care for all their neighbours in need. From the very beginning, a this-worldly and an other-worldly commitment have characterized Catholic Christianity. The ancient *Didache*, one of the earliest Christian works outside the New Testament, enjoined not only the regular practice of daily prayer (8. 3) but also generous help towards those in need (4. 5–8).

6. A Madonna and Child from Burma (Myanmar).

Over the centuries, innumerable Catholic men and women have served others through schools, colleges, hospitals, and other social ministries. In this, they have been constantly supported by communities of men and women leading lives of silence and contemplative prayer.

In modern times, devotion to God in prayer and a practical love towards others have gone hand in hand for Catholic or Catholic-inspired groups that teach in a huge variety of educational institutions, provide health care, run soup kitchens, staff leprosaria, provide dying derelicts with dignified shelter, create homes for the mentally disabled, and assist refugees and asylum-seekers (Figure 7).

Such engagement happens with significantly different emphases. Justice and Peace groups, members of Opus Dei, those who support CAFOD (the Catholic Agency for Overseas Development), the Focolare Movement, members of Christian Life Communities, lay affiliates of Carmelites and Dominicans, and other movements work, think, and pray in diverse ways. They do not live their Catholic vocation in exactly the same way. But they are all concerned to be both engaged with a suffering world and assiduous about communion with God through prayer.

Faith and reason

Catholicism has never embraced the opposition between Athens (standing for reason) and Jerusalem (standing for faith), classically expressed by Tertullian (d. around AD 225) when he denounced Greek philosophers and the heirs of Plato's Academy: 'What has Athens to do with Jerusalem? What has the Academy to do with the Church?' (*De Praescriptione Haereticorum*, 7). Through the 4th-century Cappadocians (St Basil of Caesarea, St Gregory of Nazianzus, St Gregory of Nyssa, St Macrina the Younger), such medieval writers as St Thomas Aquinas and Dante, and down to the 1998 encyclical of John Paul II, *Fides*

7. Pope John Paul II embraces Mother Teresa of Calcutta.

et Ratio ('Faith and reason'), Catholic Christianity has never accepted a separation between God's gift of faith and the cultivation of human reason.

The Cappadocians and other fathers of the Church had received an excellent education in the classics of Greek and Latin literature. When barbarian invasions tore Europe apart, monasteries of men and women in Ireland and elsewhere kept learning alive. We can recall, for example, Rosvitha, a 10th-century canoness of an abbey in Saxony. She was not only very learned in the scriptures, the writings of the fathers of the Church, and classical Latin literature, but also composed in Latin a number of plays and poems. By leading a renewal in theological learning and recovering (through Islamic and Jewish scholarship) the philosophy of Aristotle, Aquinas expressed a harmony between faith and reason. Following his lead, Dante blended human learning and divine revelation in the *Divine Comedy*. His two companions in that masterpiece were Virgil and his beloved Beatrice, the former symbolizing true humanism and the latter divine wisdom.

Occasionally, tensions grew between faith and reason or between the truths of revelation and worldly learning, above all after the rise of the natural sciences. Sometimes these conflicts arose from rational, scientific, and materialist claims to enjoy total authority over the interpretation and even the control of all reality. Sometimes Catholics, in particular Church officials, were to blame. After making the right decision to reform in 1582 the calendar of Julius Caesar, Roman authorities proved disastrously intransigent in the case of Galileo Galilei (1564–1642). Since his observations that the earth moved around the sun seemed to challenge the Church's authority to interpret the scriptures, he was forced to retract his position. His case came to symbolize for many people an antagonism between scientific reason and faith. But all truth is based in God, and there can never be final opposition between religious and scientific truths. The Austrian abbot Johann Gregor Mendel, through his experiments with peas in the monastery garden that prefigured modern genetics, in his own way symbolizes what Aquinas stood for: the basic harmony of all truth, whether known through divine revelation or human research.

That said, advances in the life sciences and technology need to be evaluated ethically and religiously; otherwise, they can threaten the dignity, environment, and even survival of the human race. With various governments increasingly ready to legalize experiments with human embryos, full and genuine dialogue between faith and scientific reason is more urgent than ever. In one of his novels, H. G. Wells (1866–1946) expressed this need by having a scientist (Dr Moreau) declare: 'I went on with this research just the way it led me...I have never troubled [myself] about the ethics of the matter' (*The Island of Dr Moreau*). Wells recognized the danger of modern science refusing to be guided by moral norms.

Further both/ands

One can pile up a long list of further both/ands that typify Catholicism: for example, both Eastern and Western ways of worship; both a cross on the tower of a church and a crucifix behind the altar; both married and celibate priests (the first being typically the case in Eastern Catholicism and the second in Western Catholicism); both bishops who come largely from the diocesan clergy (the West) and bishops who come from monastic life (the East); both the (very many) lay members and the (comparatively few) ordained ministers; both saints and sinners who belong to the same Church; both institutional structures and charismatic initiatives; both prayerful fasting during Lent and joyful feasting at Easter.

The same both/and attitude applies or, at least, should apply to the differing tendencies and methods that characterize theology: an emphasis on truth and intellectual rigour; an emphasis on worship and beauty; and an emphasis on action for justice. One might express this diversity by speaking of theologies of the head, the heart, and the hands, respectively. The first style characterizes much of European and North American theology; the second describes the theology of Eastern Catholics and other Christians; the third distinguishes liberation theology and its offshoots. A truly Catholic view of theology should be open to all three approaches.

The same kind of Catholic openness should typify attitudes towards art, architecture, and music. Catholics need both the medieval windows of Chartres Cathedral and the innovative, Chinese-style windows of the restored cathedral in Shanghai. They need both the glorious heritage of plainchant and tasteful modern hymns.

Unity

From the time of Ignatius of Antioch (d. around 107), Cyprian of Carthage (d. 258), and Augustine of Hippo (d. 430), we find Catholic Christians shrinking from divisions and sharing a gut feeling that worldwide unity must be maintained. Inevitable and healthy tensions have continued to arise between unity and diversity, and between the inherited institutions (essentially the pastoral government of bishops in communion with the bishop of Rome) and fresh movements inspired by the Holy Spirit that can bring beneficial developments in the life of the Church. Such situations are properly handled neither by an inflexible rigidity nor by a naive readiness to embrace every change. The Church at large constantly needs to apply the tests proposed by Blessed John Henry Newman (1801–90) and distinguish between faithful, life-giving developments and disloyal corruption.

In a world that now includes many separate Christian denominations, Catholics hope that new movements, led by Spirit-guided men and women, should not bring separation and any breaking of communion with others. Rather, they should enrich the whole Church, whether these movements last for only a short time or for many centuries, as was the case with the religious families founded by Benedict, Scholastica, Dominic, Francis, Clare, Ignatius Loyola, and Mary Ward.

Undoubtedly, the institutional authority of bishops has at times been exercised foolishly and sinfully against men and women who charismatically proposed fresh ideas and new commitments. But that same authority has often worked to defend and promote people raised by the Holy Spirit to minister to others in times of crisis and challenge.

The Second Vatican Council (*Gaudium et Spes*, 92) followed Pope John XXIII in endorsing the wise counsel of ancient writers: 'let there be unity in what is necessary, freedom in what is doubtful, and charity in everything (*sit in necessariis unitas, in dubiis libertas, in omnibus caritas*)'. This brings us to the agenda for Chapter 7, which will set out some of the major challenges facing the Catholic Church at the start of the third millennium.

Chapter 7
The future of Catholicism

Now we turn to the major challenges faced by Catholics and their leaders as they move further into the third millennium. Let us begin with issues of war and peace.

War and peace

From the time of Benedict XV (pope 1914–22) popes have led the world in insisting on the priority of peaceful ways over violent ways for settling international conflict. As the leading apostle of peace in the world, John Paul II stood out for his firm opposition to war, right down to his clear 'No' to the invasion of Iraq in 2003. In an address he delivered in January 2004 to the diplomats accredited to the Holy See, he once again expressed his conviction: 'war never resolves conflicts between peoples'. Pope Francis played a significant role in finally bringing some harmony between Cuba and the USA. Yet, despite the efforts of popes, of Dorothy Day, Daniel Berrigan, and other activists for peace, rethinking classical 'just-war theory' has hardly begun. In past centuries casualties were often largely confined to the soldiers and sailors of opposing armies and navies. The unjustified (or should we say criminal?) invasion of Iraq in 2003 and its horribly drawn-out aftermath (that has added millions to the refugees of war) illustrate the awful impact of modern war on civilians and their societies. The Second Vatican Council's attempt to rethink the evil of war and develop avenues of peace (*Gaudium et Spes*, 70–82) must be taken much further.

The hierarchies of power in the West focus on economic success, engender an individualism that cares little about the needy, and have few qualms about resorting to violence. Pope Francis in *Evangelii Gaudium* (52–60), *Laudato Si'* (48–52), and elsewhere has called for a return to person-centred ethics in the world of finance and economics. He has denounced unregulated markets, financial speculation, increased debt burden on poorer countries, bribery, tax evasion, and the forces that encourage a throw-away, consumerist mentality. Global inequality and injustice create the conditions for the spread of violence and war.

In *Laudato Si'* Francis called for justice towards our common home, the earth. We should be at peace and not at war with our planet. Plundering and degrading the environment and its resources constitute an ethical and religious issue, and not merely a scientific and economic problem. A satisfactory, or even a possible, existence for future human beings depends upon the present generation caring conscientiously for the planet, its living species, and the raw materials and sources of energy it provides.

In the past, Christians often pursued intolerant policies towards those they disagreed with. Nowadays in the Western world secular 'progressives' often display intolerance towards those who have reservations about embryo research, same-sex marriage, abortion, or physician-assisted suicide and who find themselves labelled bigots, out of touch with the march of history, and shouted down as not worth a hearing. Reasonable relations in society should mean refraining from dismissing those who disagree with us as stupid or wicked. The cause of peace demands civil behaviour.

Here one deplorable current is the demonizing of Muslims, which feeds off ethnic, religious, and economic prejudice. The Second Vatican Council laid a platform for relationship with Muslims in

Nostra Aetate (no. 3). But Catholics and others still have a long way to go in learning about Islam and engaging with Muslims in ways that will further a common cause on all kinds of vital issues. Ignorance of Islam and indifference to Muslims are incompatible with authentic Christian faith, as well as being highly dangerous in the contemporary world.

The family and women

The exhortation that Pope Francis published in March 2016, *Amoris Laetitia*, aimed at encouraging 'love in the family' (Figure 8). Marriage is the basis of the family, and the family is the basis for the wellbeing not only of the Catholic Church but also of society at large. In many ways the future of the family will be the future of the world. The family is the primary unit of the common good. The best economic unit any country enjoys is the family. The best welfare scheme to be promoted is the family. Yet many governments fail to give the health of family life a top priority. In my own country, Australia, domestic violence remains a widespread scourge, from which women and children primarily suffer.

Over fifty years ago the Second Vatican Council regretted that 'basic personal rights' of women are not being 'respected everywhere'. Women 'are denied the chance freely to choose a husband or a state of life, or to have access to the same educational and cultural benefits as are available to men'. Such 'forms of social or political discrimination in basic personal rights on the basis of sex' must be 'eradicated as incompatible with God's design' (*Gaudium et Spes*, 29). How many countries still fail to respect the basic rights of women? In how many more countries do women suffer from forms of 'social and political discrimination'?

In a 2013 interview with the editor of *Civiltà Cattolica*, Pope Francis said: 'it is necessary to broaden the opportunities for a

8. A christening in Roehampton, London. The water of baptism brings new life, and the Easter candle symbolizes the light of Christ who will guide the baptized.

stronger presence of women in the Church. The challenge today is this: to think about the specific place of women also in those places where the authority in the Church is exercised for various areas of the Church.' Yet over three years into his papacy what has happened, apart from five (up from three) women being nominated to a group that enjoys little influence, the International Theological Commission? The pope's special cabinet of nine male cardinals (the 'G9') has not been doubled by the addition of women to become the G18. In May 2016, however, Francis declared himself open to steps that could lead to women being ordained to the ministry of deacon. This possibility, one should recall, had been studied for years by the International Theological Commission. It produced in 2002 a document entitled *The Diaconate: Evolution and Perspectives* (so named in the original French), and left open the question of women being ordained to the diaconate.

Thus far this final chapter has been raising issues concerned with the future of humanity at large. The comments of the pope on women exercising authority brings us to challenges within the life of the Church itself.

Loss of credibility

An Oscar-winning film, *Spotlight*, turned its camera on the way bishops and others protected priests (and male religious) who sexually abused minors, instead of helping victims and implementing firm policies to prevent further crimes. A clerical 'culture', obsessed with saving 'the good name' of the Church, did not quickly call to account the perpetrators and failed to make the best interests of children its highest priority. Another recent film, *Calvary*, dramatically depicted results of this sick clericalism. Loss of credibility and trust blighted the life of a remote parish in Ireland and led to an innocent, dedicated priest being murdered.

The scandal of clerical sex abuse hit the Western world—not to mention other countries such as Chile, Paraguay, Peru, and Uruguay—at a time when sharing in the Sunday Mass has ceased to be the practice of many Catholics. Staying on the activity treadmill and cramming as much as possible into already busy schedules leave little time for the spiritual revitalization of the weekly Eucharist. In the so-called 'First World', often only a minority, week by passing week, hear the good news of the Word, receive the Bread of Life, and bond in nourishing fellowship with other Mass-goers.

In too many Western countries, laity of all ages, but especially the young, no longer regularly attend Mass on Sundays. A key challenge for the Catholic Church in these countries is to reverse the decline and effect a return to a substantial Sunday attendance at the Eucharist, 'the source and summit' of Catholic life (Vatican II, *Sacrosanctum Concilium*, 10).

At Advent 2011, church officials, after sweeping aside without any dialogue a very readable translation of the Missal already approved by the bishops of the English-speaking world in 1998, imposed on the Catholics of that world a clunky, 'Latinized' version of the liturgy. It fails to be clear and intelligible in a way that would encourage something central to the teaching of the Second Vatican Council: the full and active participation in worship of all those present. The 2011 translation, more accurately called a 'transliteralization', belongs to the current bad news. It drives people away from the Eucharist, instead of drawing them to it.

The incomparably better English of the 1998 translation is there, waiting in the wings. The bishops of the English-speaking world lost credibility when they caved in to pressure from the Vatican and introduced an allegedly 'sacral' translation. It is alien to the direct and familiar way of speaking to God practised by the psalmists and taught by Jesus himself. The present conferences of English-speaking bishops would make amends for a weak capitulation and regain some credibility if they were to put an end to a liturgical scandal by re-approving the 1998 translation.

Lay men and women

Often what harms Catholic life comes from within the Church and not from outside forces. Vatican II names the Eucharist as the source and summit of Catholic life. But in many Western countries official policies of closing parishes and refusing to ordain mature, married men is depriving more and more Catholics of the life-giving power of the Eucharist, the powerful point of unity for their faith. The Church is where the Eucharist is, and the Eucharist forms the Church—to echo the 2003 encyclical of John Paul II, *Ecclesia de Eucharistia* ('the Church from the Eucharist'). Far too many Catholics are unable, Sunday by Sunday, to share the Eucharist, find in it the centre of their existence, and draw from it the strength and light they need for their lives.

A very serious priest shortage threatens the Eucharistic life of the Church. The local community has a right to the regular celebration of the Eucharist. In an article originally published in 1977, Karl Rahner wrote: 'provision for sufficiently large numbers of pastoral clergy is an obligation imposed on the Church as a matter of divine law, an obligation that takes precedence in a case of conflict over the Church's legitimate desire for a celibate pastoral clergy'.

Cardinal Karl Lehmann, who was the chairman of the German Bishops' Conference for twenty years, called for a 'mental revolution' in the Church vis-à-vis married priests and the ordination of women. Such a mental revolution is needed above all in the case of the bishops. For years now the majority of lay people have shown themselves open to these two changes.

Women continue to be excluded from the ordained ministry (even from ordination to the diaconate) and from positions of official leadership in the Church. Yet across the world, Catholic women have persistently provided education, health care, and various social services. They often lead the way in supporting families and children; in caring for single parents, refugees, and those in foster care or prison; in working for those suffering from various disabilities and crises of mental health; in helping those who need housing, supported accommodation, age care facilities, and retirement homes. In Australia, challenges in the 1965–80 period had brought the Catholic school system to the brink. Largely led by lay people, with women the driving force, the Church responded courageously, transformed Catholic education, and made it stronger than ever. What women have done in education and other fields promises well for what they would contribute to a full partnership with bishops, priests, religious, and lay men.

The laws and customs of the Church must be reviewed and modified to achieve such a partnership in leading and facilitating the full life of the Church in parishes, dioceses, and nations. The presence of women with appropriate authority on the diocesan and national level would, for instance, undoubtedly help implement policies and practices that prevent sexual and physical abuse of young people in the care of the Church. The effective presence of women could overcome the crisis of credibility that Church leaders face.

The global Church

Since 1989 the global South has enjoyed more Catholics than the global North. Today there are more Catholics in Africa than in the whole of Europe. Although accurate statistics may be hard to come by, it appears to be true that on Sundays more Christians worship in China than in all Europe. The proud claim made by Hilaire Belloc (d. 1953), 'Europe is the faith and the faith is Europe', has become utterly implausible today.

In the Catholic Church too much power continues to be centralized in the Vatican. Add to this that over 60 per cent of the cardinals who voted in the last papal conclave (March 2013) came from Europe and North America. Pope Francis obviously set himself to decentralize decision-making and to make the college of cardinals correspond more fairly to the actual composition of the worldwide Catholic Church.

Western Catholics, as much as ever, are encountering the rest of the world—not least through a kind of 'reverse mission'. In Australia, Canada, Germany, the USA, and elsewhere, more and more priests from India, Nigeria, Vietnam, and other non-First World countries are staffing parishes.

Nowadays the churches of the First World have to listen rather than to speak, to learn rather than to teach. Let me offer two examples. First, Catholics and other Christians in non-First World countries lead the way in the practice of popular religion (through song, dance, processions, celebration of saints, and the rest). Popular religion has proved its power to connect with people's lives. It could enrich enormously the liturgy and life of First World Christians.

Second, First World countries are faced with the growing presence of Muslims, Hindus, Buddhists, and followers of other non-Christian, world religions. Asia, the birthplace of these religions, has learned to deal appropriately with religious diversity, as well as experiencing at times tragic breakdowns in relations between those of different faiths. Asian Catholics and other Christians have much to teach their First World counterparts not only about coping with religious diversity but also about being enriched by it.

Conclusion

The famous words with which Charles Dickens opened *A Tale of Two Cities*, 'the best of times and the worst of times', focus the present state of the Catholic Church around the world. In the early third millennium, those who lead Catholic dioceses and parishes, teach and study in Catholic schools and colleges, administer and work for Catholic hospitals, or in other sectors share closely in the life of the Church constantly face the best of news and the worst of

9. Pope Francis welcomes refugees from Syria.

news. They continue to bless the world in numerous ways. Yet very many of them are aware that serious reform at every level is needed to meet pressing challenges and make the Church a much richer blessing to all nations.

The whole Church is called to a radical conversion to the living Christ. Experiencing him deeply can enable Catholics not only to renew their own fellowship in the life of the Church but also to work for the common good of all men and women. More than ever the human race needs Catholics and other Christians whose lives are totally centred on Jesus and joyfully ready to care for those who suffer. In *Evangelii Gaudium* ('the Joy of the Gospel'), Pope Francis (Figure 9) spelled out in detail the real happiness that a renewed personal encounter with Jesus will bring. That exhortation could prove a magna carta for a new age of Catholicism.

Timeline

1274	Death of St Thomas Aquinas
1321	Death of Dante Alighieri
1450	Johannes Gutenberg creates the printing press
1453	Constantinople falls to the Turks
1492	Christopher Columbus discovers America
1498	Vasco da Gama reaches Kerala (India) and meets St Thomas Christians
1517	Martin Luther publishes his ninety-five theses
1545–63	Council of Trent
1556	Death of St Ignatius Loyola
1582	Death of St Teresa of Avila
1640	Death of Matteo Ricci in Beijing
1704	Pope Clement XI condemns 'Chinese Rites'
1776	American Declaration of Independence
1789	Start of French Revolution
1815	Death of Archbishop John Carroll
1846–78	Papacy of Blessed Pius IX
1869/70	First Vatican Council
1890	Death of Blessed John Henry Newman
1914–18	First World War
1939–45	Second World War
1958–63	Papacy of St John XXIII
1962–5	Second Vatican Council
1963–78	Papacy of Blessed Paul VI
1978–2005	Papacy of St John Paul II
2005–13	Papacy of Benedict XVI
March 2013–	Papacy of Francis

Further reading

Sources

St Thomas Aquinas, *Summa Theologiae*, trans. T. Gilby et al., 61 vols (London: Eyre & Spottiswoode, 1964–6).

James Buckley et al. (eds), *The Blackwell Companion to Catholicism* (Oxford: Blackwell, 2007).

Catechism of the Catholic Church (Vatican City: Libreria Editrice Vaticana, 1992; various editions of the English translation).

F. L. Cross and E. A. Livingstone (eds), *The Oxford Dictionary of the Christian Church*, 4th edn (Oxford: Oxford University Press, 2006).

Heinrich Denzinger and Peter Hünermann, *Enchiridion Symbolorum, Definitionum et Declarationum*, 43rd edn (San Francisco: Ignatius Press, 2012).

Erwin Fahlbusch et al., *The Encyclopedia of Christianity*, 5 vols (Grand Rapids, Mich.: Eerdmans, 1999–2008).

Philippe Levillain (ed.), *The Papacy: An Encyclopedia*, 3 vols (London: Routledge, 2003).

Josef Neuner and Jacques Dupuis (eds), *The Christian Faith*, 7th edn (Bangalore/New York: Theological Publications in India/Alba House, 2001).

New Catholic Encyclopedia, 15 vols, 2nd edn (Washington, DC: Catholic University of America, 2003).

Karl Rahner, *Theological Investigations*, 23 vols (London: Darton, Longman & Todd, 1961–92).

Norman Tanner (ed.), *Decrees of the Ecumenical Councils*, 2 vols (London: Sheed & Ward, 1990).

General

Karl Adam, *The Spirit of Catholicism* (London: Sheed & Ward, 1929).

Dante Alighieri, *The Divine Comedy*, trans. Robin Kirkpatrick, 3 vols (London: Penguin, 2006–7).

John L. Allen, *The Catholic Church: What Everyone Needs to Know* (New York: Oxford University Press, 2013).

Henri de Lubac, *Catholicism: Christ and the Common Destiny of Man* (San Francisco: Ignatius Press, 1988).

Richard P. McBrien, *Catholicism*, 2nd edn (San Francisco: Harper San Francisco, 1994).

Gerald O'Collins, *Living Vatican II: The 21st Council for the 21st Century* (Mahwah, NJ: Paulist Press, 2006).

Gerald O'Collins and Mario Farrugia, *Catholicism: The Story of Catholic Christianity*, 2nd edn (Oxford: Oxford University Press, 2015).

Karl Rahner, *The Foundations of Christian Faith* (New York: Crossroad, 1978).

Joseph Ratzinger, *Introduction to Christianity* (New York: Herder & Herder, 1969).

Roderick Strange, *The Catholic Faith* (London: Darton, Longman & Todd, 2001).

Chapter 1: From Pentecost to Christopher Columbus (AD 30–1492)

Peter Brown, *The Rise of Western Christendom: Triumph and Diversity A.D. 200–1000* (Oxford: Blackwell, 1996).

Henry Chadwick, *The Church in Ancient Society: From Galilee to Gregory the Great* (Oxford: Clarendon Press, 2001).

Angelo Di Berardino et al. (eds), *Encyclopedia of Ancient Christianity*, 3 vols (Downers Grove, Ill.: IVP Academic, 2014).

Eamon Duffy, *Saints and Sinners: A History of the Popes* (New Haven, Conn.: Yale University Press, 1997).

Adrian Hastings (ed.), *A World History of Christianity* (London: Cassell, 1999).

Judith M. Lieu, *Marcion and the Making of a Heretic* (Cambridge: Cambridge University Press, 2015).

Diarmaid N. J. MacCulloch, *A History of Christianity: The First Two Thousand Years* (London: Allen Lane, 2013).

Edward Norman, *The Roman Catholic Church: An Illustrated History* (London: Thames and Hudson, 2007).

David S. Potter, *Constantine the Emperor* (New York: Oxford University Press, 2012).

Diana Webb, *Pilgrims and Pilgrimages in the Medieval West* (London: Tauris, 1999).

Chapter 2: From Christopher Columbus to the present (1492–2017)

Giuseppe Alberigo and Joseph A. Komonchak (eds), *History of Vatican II*, 5 vols (Maryknoll, NY: Orbis, 1996–2006).

Robert Bireley, *The Refashioning of Catholicism 1450–1700* (Basingstoke: Macmillan, 1999).

David G. Dalin, *The Myth of Hitler's Pope* (Washington, DC: Regnery, 2005).

Adrian Hastings, *The Church in Africa 1450–1950* (Oxford: Oxford University Press, 1994).

Hans J. Hillerbrand (ed.), *The Oxford Encyclopedia of the Reformation*, 4 vols (Oxford: Oxford University Press, 1996).

Alberto Melloni et al. (eds), *Vatican II: The Complete History* (Mahwah, NJ: Paulist Press, 2015).

Sally Ninham, *Ten African Cardinals* (Brisbane/Leominster: Connor Court/Gracewing, 2014).

Gerald O'Collins, *On the Left Bank of the Tiber* (Brisbane/Leominister: Connor Court/Gracewing, 2013).

Gerald O'Collins, *From Rome to Royal Park* (Brisbane/Leominster: Connor Court/Gracewing, 2015).

Mark Riebling, *Church of Spies: The Pope's Secret War Against Hitler* (New York: Basic Books, 2015).

Charles Taylor, *A Secular Age* (Cambridge, Mass.: Harvard University Press, 2007).

Chapter 3: Catholics on God and the human condition

Lewis Ayres, *Nicaea and its Legacy* (Oxford: Oxford University Press, 2004).

Yves Congar, *I Believe in the Holy Spirit*, 3 vols (London: Geoffrey Chapman, 1983).

Stephen T. Davis et al. (eds), *The Trinity* (Oxford: Oxford University Press, 1999).

Stephen T. Davis et al. (eds), *The Incarnation* (Oxford: Oxford University Press, 2001).

Piet F. Fransen, *The New Life of Grace* (New York: Seabury Press, 1973).

Francesca Aran Murphy (ed.), *The Oxford Handbook of Christology* (Oxford: Oxford University Press, 2015).

Gerald O'Collins, *Christology*, 2nd edn (Oxford: Oxford University Press, 2009).

Gerald O'Collins, *Jesus our Redeemer: A Christian Approach to Salvation* (Oxford: Oxford University Press, 2007).

Gerald O'Collins, *Revelation: Towards a Christian Interpretation of God's Self-Revelation in Jesus Christ* (Oxford: Oxford University Press, 2016).

Gerald O'Collins, *The Tripersonal God*, 2nd edn (Mahwah, NJ: Paulist Press, 2014).

Chapter 4: The sacraments and the Catholic Church

Louis-Marie Chauvet, *The Sacraments* (Collegeville, Minn.: Liturgical Press, 2001).

Avery Dulles, *Models of the Church*, 2nd edn (Maryknoll, NY: Orbis, 1992).

Kevin W. Irwin, *The Sacraments* (Mahwah, NJ: Paulist Press, 2015).

Maxwell E. Johnson, *The Rites of Christian Initiation: Their Evolution and Interpretation* (Collegeville, Minn.: Liturgical Press, 1999).

Walter Kasper, *The Catholic Church: Nature, Reality, and Mission* (London: T. & T. Clark, 2015).

Richard P. McBrien, *The Church: The Evolution of Catholicism* (New York: HarperOne, 2008).

Enrico Massa, *The Celebration of the Eucharist: The Origin of the Rite and the Development of its Interpretation* (Collegeville, Minn.: Pueblo, 1999).

K. Schatz, *Papal Primacy from its Origins to the Present* (Collegeville, Minn.: Liturgical Press, 1996).

Chapter 5: Catholic moral life and teaching

Pope Francis, *Laudato Si'* (Vatican City: Libreria Editrice Vaticana, 2015; other editions available).

Pope Francis, *Amoris Laetitia* (Vatican City: Libreria Editrice Vaticana, 2016; other editions available).

Pope John Paul II, *Veritatis Splendor* (Vatican City: Libreria Editrice Vaticana, 1993; other editions available).

James F. Keenan, *A History of Catholic Moral Theology in the Twentieth Century* (London: Continuum, 2000).

John Mahoney, *The Making of Moral Theology: A Study of the Roman Catholic Tradition* (Oxford: Clarendon Press, 1989).

John T. Noonan, Jr, *A Church That Can and Cannot Change: The Development of Catholic Moral Teaching* (Notre Dame, Ind.: University of Notre Dame Press, 2005).

The Second Vatican Council, *Gaudium et Spes* (Vatican City: Libreria Editrice Vaticana, 1966; other editions available).

Chapter 6: Characteristics of Catholicism

Thomas Bamat and Jean-Paul Wiest (eds), *Popular Catholicism in a World Church: Seven Case Studies in Inculturation* (Maryknoll, NY: Orbis, 1999).

Sarah Jane Boss (ed.), *Mary: The Complete Resource* (London: Continuum, 2007).

Caroline H. Ebertshäuser et al. (eds), *Mary: Art, Culture, and Religion through the Ages* (New York: Crossroad, 1998).

John Henry Newman, *An Essay on the Development of Christian Doctrine* (Harmondsworth: Penguin, 1974).

Gerald O'Collins and Edward G. Farrugia, *A Concise Dictionary of Theology*, 3rd edn (Mahwah, NJ: Paulist Press, 2013).

Chapter 7: The future of Catholicism

William D'Antonio and Anthony Pogorelc (eds), *Voices of the Faithful: Loyal Catholics Striving for Change* (New York: Herder & Herder, 2007).

Jacques Dupuis, *Christianity and the Religions* (Maryknoll, NY: Orbis, 2002).

Pope Francis, *Evangelii Gaudium* (Vatican City: Libreria Editrice Vaticana, 2013; other editions available).

Philip Jenkins, *The Next Christendom: The Coming of Global Christianity*, 3rd edn (New York: Oxford University Press, 2011).

Piero Marini, *A Challenging Reform: Realizing the Vision of Liturgical Renewal* (Dublin: Columba Press, 2007).

Gerald O'Collins, *Salvation for All: God's Other Peoples* (Oxford: Oxford University Press, 2008).

John Quinn, *The Reform of the Papacy* (New York: Crossroad, 1999).

Index

Catholicism

SOCIAL MEDIA
Very Short Introduction

Join our community

www.oup.com/vsi

- Join us online at the official Very Short Introductions **Facebook** page.
- Access the thoughts and musings of our authors with our online **blog**.
- Sign up for our monthly **e-newsletter** to receive information on all new titles publishing that month.
- Browse the full range of Very Short Introductions online.
- Read **extracts** from the Introductions for free.
- If you are a teacher or lecturer you can order inspection copies quickly and simply via our website.

ONLINE
CATALOGUE
A Very Short Introduction

Our online catalogue is designed to make it easy to find your ideal Very Short Introduction. View the entire collection by subject area, watch author videos, read sample chapters, and download reading guides.

http://global.oup.com/uk/academic/general/vsi_list/

KABBALAH
A Very Short Introduction
Joseph Dan

In *Kabbalah*, Joseph Dan debunks the myths surrounding modern Kabbalistic practice, offering an engaging and dependable account of this traditional Jewish religious phenomenon and its impact outside of Judaism. Dan sheds light on the many misconceptions about what Kabbalah is and isn't—including its connections to magic, astronomy, alchemy, and numerology—and he illuminates the relationship between Kabbalah and Christianity on the one hand and New Age religion on the other. Dan examines its fascinating historical background, including key ancient texts of this tradition. He concludes with a brief survey of scholarship in the field and a list of books for further reading.

> "Dan has given us the best concise history of Jewish mysticism. . . . As a 'very short introduction' to this sublime treasure house, Joseph Dan's book is warmly recommended."
>
> Benjamin Balint, Commentary

PURITANISM
A Very Short Introduction
Francis J. Bremer

Written by a leading expert on the Puritans, this brief, informative volume offers a wealth of background on this key religious movement. This book traces the shaping, triumph, and decline of the Puritan world, while also examining the role of religion in the shaping of American society and the role of the Puritan legacy in American history. Francis J. Bremer discusses the rise of Puritanism in the English Reformation, the struggle of the reformers to purge what they viewed as the corruptions of Roman Catholicism from the Elizabethan church, and the struggle with the Stuart monarchs that led to a brief Puritan triumph under Oliver Cromwell.

www.oup.com/vsi

Mormonism
A Very Short Introduction
Richard Lyman Bushman

Mormonism is frequently described as the most successful
indigenous American religion. Mormon beliefs arouse curiosity
because they depart from normal Christian doctrine, leading
to the question: Are Mormons Christian? This introduction
will include the history of the contemporary Mormonism,
and an analysis and emphasis of Mormon beliefs, beginning
with Joseph Smith, the founding prophet.

www.oup.com/vsi